The Lunchbox Mama

RACHEL STIRLING

Black&White

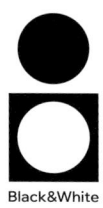
Black & White

First published in the UK in 2024 by
Black & White Publishing Ltd
Nautical House, 104 Commercial Street, Edinburgh, EH6 6NF

A division of Bonnier Books UK
4th Floor, Victoria House, Bloomsbury Square, London, WC1B 4DA
Owned by Bonnier Books
Sveavägen 56, Stockholm, Sweden

Copyright © Rachel Stirling 2024

All rights reserved. No part of this publication may be reproduced, stored or transmitted in any form by any means, electronic, mechanical, photocopying or otherwise, without the prior written permission of the publisher.

The right of Rachel Stirling to be identified as Author of this work has been asserted by her in accordance with the Copyright, Designs and Patents Act, 1988.

All photography copyright © Susie Lowe
Illustrations on chapter openers © Shutterstock/Beskova Ekaterina
Illustrations on pages 22-3, 152-3 by Tonje Hefte

The publisher has made every reasonable effort to contact copyright holders of material in this book. Any errors are inadvertent and anyone who for any reason has not been contacted is invited to write to the publisher so that a full acknowledgement can be made in subsequent editions of this work.

A CIP catalogue record for this book is available from the British Library.

ISBN: 978 1 78530 583 2

1 3 5 7 9 10 8 6 4 2

Layout by Richard Budd.
Printed and bound in Latvia.

www.blackandwhitepublishing.com

Goodness, I really love your account!! As well as marvellous lunch ideas, you are so encouraging and make everybody (well, me) feel like my best is good enough. Thank you! - Helen

It's made me think about savvy food storage! - Ola

Smart, creative and fun lunchbox ideas that keep my kiddies interested and well fed - Vicky

Awesome

I love how my mummy cuts my food into different shapes - Heath, age 7

My daughter's packed lunchbox used to come home barely touched most days but your ideas have made lunchtime fun for her and the box comes home completely empty!! - Kate

Your page is a lifesaver for packed lunch ideas! - Clare

My 4-year-old never ate her packed lunch until I started prettying up her sandwiches - Kiiran

Genius ideas from a relatable mum - what's not to love?! Packed lunches for my 3-year-old definitely went up a level after I started following you, thank you! - Tori

We came across the page by chance and love it! There are so many exciting snack ideas that we have already done with our children or have saved to do in the future! - Kerry

Fun and exciting, she never seems to run out of ideas! - Elliot age 9

You're awesome and awe inspiring - Sophie

I can make lunch more exciting and appealing for my 4-year-old, she has T1D so it's important she eats what I've made her at the childminder's - Becca

I used to dread packed lunches until Rachel came into my life, now lunches are creative and my daughter is always excited to see what delights are in her lunchbox - Rachel

Oh wow, I just want to say I love your page and it's helped my 5-year-old autistic son try new foods. Even school mentioned how cool his lunches are. Your page has helped so much! - Becky

Amazing ideas

This book is dedicated to my two amazing children. Without you, none of this would have been possible.

Contents

Introduction	1
A Note on Fussy Eaters	2
A Note on Safety	3
Why Packed Lunches?	5
Budget Friendly Lunches	6
Lunchbox Essentials	8
Kitchen Essentials	12
The Lunchbox Formula	15
Store Cupboard Essentials	16
The Fussy Eater Cheat Sheet	17
So, What's Next?	21

The Lunchboxes

Easy Wins

Cucumber Crowns	26
Love Heart Strawberries	28
Veggie Cutters	29
Heart Cocktail Sausages & Mini Carrots	31
Food Picks	32
Spotty Dino Eggs	32
Heart Eggs	34
DIY Dippers	35
Jelly in the Box	37
Sandwich Pockets	38
Chocolate Spread Hack	39
Pepperoni Roses	41

Starting the Week Strong

Sandwich Roll-Ups	44
Peek-a-Boo Sandwiches	46
Shape Cutters	48
Sausage Roll-Ups	50
Sandwich Kebabs	53
Sandwich Sunshines	55
Cold Toasties	57
Omelette Wraps	59
DIY Fajita Lunch	61
Mega Sandwich Swirls	62
A Note on Crusts	63

End of the Week

Pizza Quesadillas	67	Porridge Flapjacks	77
Cheese Toastie Roll-Ups	69	Kiddie Charcuterie	79
Mini Hot Dogs	71	Easy Peasy Cheesy Scones	81
Pancake Lunchables	72	Garlic Toast Bites	83
Nacho Average Thursday	75	Cheat Sausage Rolls	85

Themed Lunches

Valentine´s Day	88	Christmas Cracker	100
Happy Birthday	91	Pirates Ahoy!	103
Easter Eggstravaganza	94	Over the Rainbow	105
Haunted Halloween	96	Ready, Steady, Go!	107
First Day of School	99	Unicorn Magic	109

School Holiday Lunches

Mini Pancake Muffins	112	Hidden Veggie Sausage Swirls	123
Jam Donut Roll-Ups	115	Toaster Wraps	124
Easy DIY Pizza Bar	117	Rainbow Toasties	125
The Sandwich Express	118	How to Platter Anything and Everything	126
Muffin Tray Lunch	121		

Fun at Home

Playdate Platters	131	Snack Necklace	143
Pick 'n' Mix Snack Bar	133	Lazy Baking	144
Snowman Hot Chocolate	134	Rainbow Toast	145
Movie Afternoon Snacks	137	Chocolate Lollies	146
Broken Biscuit Rocky Road	138	The Happiest of Meals	149
Any Excuse for a Tea Party	140		

Introduction

I can't believe I'm sitting here writing a book. An actual book! I don't think this was ever part of the plan – in fact, I don't think I ever had a plan. All I did have was a fussy eater and a need to feed him and keep him alive!

So, hello! I'm Rachel, mum of two and wife of one, and known to my Instagram family as The Lunchbox Mama. I started my page in summer 2019 just as my boy, now ten, was finishing his first year of school.

I want this book to be the resource I never had when I suddenly had to start producing packed lunches every morning. I felt the pressure to make my son a lunch that would fill him and fuel him for the afternoon, while also knowing that he was quite a fussy eater who didn't do well with a boring hunk of sandwich.

So, I hope that now this book will sit on your shelf and be the ideas your brain hasn't got time to think of. For you to be able to pull it out on a Monday morning after a busy family weekend and instantly have some easy ideas you can pack into your children's lunchboxes – in among the usual chaos of getting kids out the door to school and (hopefully) with some shred of sanity left.

The mental load of feeding our kids is huge, and I manage better when I have a plan. BUT when it comes to feeding fussy eaters, I've never found other people's plans to be that helpful: there's always some ideas that won't work for me and my family. For this reason, I haven't made firm plans here – instead I've split my ideas into chapters in a way I hope will help you most. There's a chapter for the start of the week – or whichever days you have fresh bread and a fridge full of lunch options – and then another chapter for the end of the week – when supplies are running low and you need to do another shop, but there hasn't been time.

We've got a chapter of easy wins, which are great when you want to mix things up a bit but haven't got time for a whole new lunch idea. But we also have my favourite kind of lunches – themed lunches. These are one hundred per cent optional, but I promise you they're so much fun! Whether you want a special birthday lunch, something festive for that school Christmas dinner day, or a themed lunch 'just because', I hope there is something for everyone in that chapter.

I've added a chapter on feeding the kids during the school holidays, because they seem to come around with alarming regularity and it's not always easy to think straight when faced with a constant barrage of snack requests! And finally, a chapter of snacktivities. These are great activities to pass the time and do something fun together, but they also double as a snack afterwards, so helpfully – and hopefully – they kill two birds with one stone! These are perfect for rainy days stuck at home, or when you feel the call to be a fun mum (but, preferably, without too much effort).

So, grab a cuppa and flick through, maybe with a notepad handy to jot down ideas for next week (there's a link to printable planners on page 21), or find some post-its and ask the kids to stick them in as bookmarks on the lunchboxes they'd like to try . . . I find if they've chosen something themselves, they're much more likely to eat it.

Tuck in. I hope you love this Lunchbox Mama book!

A Note on Fussy Eaters

While I hope this book will be helpful for all families packing lunches in the primary school years, I really want it to help those of you trying to feed a fussy eater. I was a fussy eater myself and ate the same lunch every day of primary school but, rest assured, I eat perfectly normally now. This gives me reassurance that if I can outgrow my fussy eating, then my children can, and will, too. But it also gives me real insight into the feelings of anxiety that some children have over trying new foods, and so my approach to fussy eating aims to respect this and work alongside the child, rather than taking the view that my job is to just 'make' them eat it.

We all have massively different ideas of what constitutes a fussy eater, and I'm not going to set out to offer a definition here, instead I want to say I GET IT! It's hard. But there are some things that can slowly help bring your child along on their fussy eater journey, rather than feeling like you're stuck in the same spot, or even going backwards.

Firstly, please remember that a fussy phase is oh so common, and secondly please know that there is even an evolutionary reason for it. Back when we were cave people, living as hunters and gatherers, children needed to be wired in such a way that they wouldn't wander off, pluck random berries and eat them. Those random berries could kill them. So next time your child is wary and untrusting of a new food you place in front of them, remember that fact! It's not (just) them being stubborn and refusing to try – instead, it's that their brain is actually programmed that way. Their wiring is making them stop, making them consider rather than diving straight in.

Sadly, this cave baby brain isn't brilliantly helpful in the twenty-first century, but you're not going to undo thousands of years of evolutionary wiring by getting cross and 'making' them eat it. So instead, I decided to have some fun. To work out ways of showing those cave baby brains that it's not only safe to try new foods – but that they can be super tasty and super fun too.

By keeping the mood light, you help keep your child's brain in a normal, calm state. If you become frustrated your child can tell: they feel stressed, cortisol starts coursing through their body, then they're on high alert for danger. Chances are, by that point, you've already lost the battle.

For this reason, re-naming foods to something your child finds comforting and safe can really help. At three years old, my son would refuse meatballs for tea, but he would eat sausage lollipops – I just stuck the meatballs on sticks! Cauliflower was white broccoli (as he was one of those few toddlers who actually liked broccoli). Oh, and he wouldn't touch soup, but he would have some 'dip-dip' if we put a tiny amount in an egg cup and gave him some toast soldiers like a boiled egg.

I find that shifting from battle-mode to challenge-mode in your own brain can help you think of fun and effective ways to win together rather than being overwhelmed by that feeling of frustration when they refuse to even try the food you've created for them (especially when we're just trying to keep them alive!).

And remember, when it comes to lunches at school: a jam sandwich in their tummies is better than a chicken sandwich that doesn't get touched and is brought back home with a hungry child. Above all, kids need food in their bellies to thrive, play and learn throughout the school day. You have multiple other occasions to get the nutrition they need into them, so if they're firmly in a jam sandwich phase, please cut yourself some slack and work with what you've got. Add what goodness you can to that jam sandwich (perhaps with 50/50 bread, or a lower sugar jam, or check out the chocolate spread hack on page 39 and do the same with jam).

But ultimately you have to pick your battles and allow both you and your fussy eater some time to come through to the other side. So much fussy eating is a phase and will (I promise) get better in time and through gentle perseverance.

Equally, if you have genuine concerns about a child's very limited eating, or any concerns about their growth or development, then it's always worth seeking reassurance from professionals. Your GP is an excellent place to start with this.

A Note on Safety

An essential DO and an essential DON'T

DO be aware of any foods considered a choke hazard. If you have younger children, especially aged six and under, make sure you cut up anything small and round; think of anything around the size of grapes or hot dogs and slice them lengthways, but also be aware of light foods like popcorn which can get stuck in airways. If in doubt, cut it up for lunches at school and practise eating them safely at home under close supervision.

DON'T add raw meats to recipes that don't cook long enough for the meat to cook through – e.g. as a pizza topping, or in omelette wraps (see page 59). If in doubt cook it through first.

Allergies and intolerances

I want this book to be as inclusive as possible, and I know what it's like to be an allergy mum. Both of my children had CMPA (cow's milk protein allergy) as babies and toddlers, and I am gluten intolerant, so I know the life of checking the back of the pack of everything you buy! The lunchbox ideas in this book are deliberately not too rigidly specific in terms of ingredients because I want everyone to be able to tailor each idea to work for their family. It's for this reason that I haven't marked them with GF or DF etc, because each idea should be easily adaptable by using your safe breads and/or sandwich fillers.

Why Packed Lunches?

I'm asked this a lot, and I get it; it's a lot of extra work, especially if your child receives a free school meal.

BUT just because it's easier and it's cheaper, it doesn't mean you have to do it if it's not right for you and your child.

If you have a child who will happily skip into school and eat what's on the school-dinner menu, then perfect, crack on! But if you have a child who is perhaps a fussy eater, or struggles with anxiety in their school day anyway, and you know that expecting them to line up and ask for their meal, then sit and eat something unfamiliar is too much right now, then don't do it.

My son was a summer baby and so he started school at only just four years old, and he wasn't ready in a lot of ways. He had his own struggles, and I knew that school dinners would only add to this. So, I made the decision to take that off his plate, as it were.

Instead, I used lunches as a little reminder of home. I used to imagine him opening his lunchbox and seeing his favourite dinosaur sandwiches and being able to eat without worry. There's not a lot of control within the school day for our children – so if this gives them a moment of control in the middle of their day, and you can make it work for your family and your budget, then do that. You can always start with packed lunches and gradually expose them to school dinners, as they become more settled and confident at school.

It could also be worth a conversation with your child's teacher. After a few weeks, you could mention that you'd like them to be given the option of trying a school dinner, perhaps alongside their packed lunch. Different schools will deal with this differently, but if you don't ask the question, they can't help.

And remember, every child is different, and that's okay.

My eldest had packed lunches five days a week in reception. Tried and liked fish and chips on Fridays in Year 1, so added that to the mix. And by Years 3 and 4 he was having two or three hot dinners a week. My youngest has just finished Year 2 and still the idea of school food fills her with anxiety. So, we don't push. She loves everything else about school and I know if I insisted she tried school dinners, then she would struggle to even go to school. So, I take the wins where we have them, and give her control over the things that she needs control over (just like an adult would do for themselves).

Budget Friendly Lunches

I wanted to include a chapter of lunch ideas for the end of the month, when the budget can be tighter, but you still need to feed everyone. But then I realised that most of the packed lunches I make are already pretty budget friendly. So, instead, here are some things I keep in mind when shopping, to help save the pennies when I'm packing lunches.

Five top tips for saving money on your food shop

1. **Look at the price per gram** part of the ticket on the supermarket shelf, so you can compare prices like for like. Don't just assume that the lowest overall price is the best value, because it might be a much smaller container.

2. **Shop the offers when you can.** If the kids love a particular food (especially a long-life snack), then only buy it when it's on offer, but buy a few packs and stash them away. Don't then decide you've got loads so they can binge through them all, but (if you have space) create your own mini back-up store cupboard, so when you run out you can go there and grab another that you bought at half price, rather than having to run out and buy it again now it's back to full price.

3. **Your freezer is your friend!** If you can buy a larger pack and freeze some, then that often works out better value than buying a small pack more often.

- For example, my kids love a cocktail sausage in their lunches. But (a) I don't want them eating processed meat every day while they use up a whole packet and (b) when they're on offer the ginormous pack of 70-something sausages is cheaper than the smaller pack of 25. So, I buy the big pack and put enough for a couple of days in an airtight tub in the fridge, then put the rest in the freezer. You can either defrost a few overnight in the fridge for the following day, or pack them from frozen to defrost in their lunchboxes by lunchtime. If you're worried about them not defrosting in time, slice them through lengthways and leave them out of the fridge while you pack the rest of the lunchbox and they'll be almost defrosted by the time you pack them up.

- The same is true for bread products where you never use the full pack. Within a couple of days of opening, make sure to chuck the rest of the packet in the freezer, and next time you need a couple of wraps, slices of bread or pitta breads for a lunch idea, you'll have them on hand.

4. **Don't buy multipacks.** Instead of buying a multipack of six mini bags of biscuits, grab one pack of the full-size biscuits, often for less than a quarter of the price. Not only is this better for the environment, it's much better for your budget too. Usually, the weight of two normal-sized biscuits is about the same as all the mini ones in a pack, plus you'll

probably get more than six servings, making them significantly cheaper per gram. And if you're using a bento box, you're probably going to tip them all out of the packet anyway! If you do need them in packets, pop them in reusable snack pouches (recommendations on page 12) at the start of the week and then they're in easy-to-grab, individual bags ready when you need a snack double quick.

5. **Make your own DIY version.** If money is tight, then the easiest way to save is to do one of the steps yourself. Instead of buying pre-sliced cheese for sandwiches, cut or grate it yourself. Instead of buying those little jelly pots, buy a ready to mix packet or block and make it yourself — you can serve the set jelly in reusable sealed tubs with a small spoon or even pour it directly into their lunchbox, and let it set there — though only if your lunchbox is definitely, absolutely leakproof!

Spot the difference: good value versus cheap

It's worth being aware that some cheaper products are made with cheaper, lower quality ingredients. Not always, but it's worth being aware. Flip the packet over and check the ingredients. If it's a list of ingredients that you recognise the names of as something you might buy — tomatoes, cheese, flour and so on — then you're good to go, but if it's full of words you might struggle to pronounce, then buy it sometimes and buy it when the budget requires it, but be aware that when you have the means you might want to mix it up and buy a more expensive, less processed option.

For example, my son loves a croissant sandwich in his lunchbox. I used to regularly buy those bags of cheap supermarket budget-branded croissants, but a quick check of the back of the pack one day really shocked me. Now I buy them less often, but when I do, I spend a bit more and get the 'all butter' version — still supermarket own brand, but far fewer processed ingredients.

Equally, if your fussy eater won't eat a less processed option, that's a battle only you can pick, but remember you are the one who decides how often you serve your child that food and you are the one who controls when and how often to mix it up with other things you'd rather they ate. I don't want to sound like a know-it-all — I honestly don't have all the answers — and I know there are days when we all serve foods we might wish we didn't serve so often. But that's life, especially a busy family life with a fussy eater (or more) thrown into the mix.

The point is for you to remember this is YOUR family and YOU are the adult, so you get to set — and adapt and revisit — the rules for your family. Food can be such a pleasure for everyone as a family, but also such a source of difficult emotions and practicalities too — still, I genuinely believe that we are all just doing our best. And the more ideas and resources we have to hand to help us with this, the better. And that's what I hope this book will help with.

Lunchbox Essentials

They say a bad workman blames their tools. Well, the same is true for lunchboxes . . . Except it really is the bad lunchbox's fault!

If you don't want to spend your mornings scrapping around for tiny tubs and lost lids, invest in a good quality bento box with lots of sections all in one place – it's a gamechanger, I promise.

Which Lunchbox?

The box you choose will be a personal choice, but here are five key questions to consider.

1. **Plastic or metal?** There are advantages to both, as long as if you choose plastic, you make sure it's good quality, BPA-free plastic. Plastic lunchboxes are often easier to buy, more cost effective, and come in fun colours that children might find more appealing. On the other hand, metal boxes have none of the risks of chemical leaching; but I haven't found one with individually sealed sections that I love, yet . . .

2. **How will you wash it?** If you intend to use the dishwasher, make sure to check whether your preferred style is dishwasher-friendly when researching which box to buy.

3. **How much food will it hold? How long will it last my child?** The bigger the box, the more it will hold, but you also don't want to be sending a cumbersome, half-empty box for years while your child's appetite grows into it.

4. **How much to spend on a lunchbox?** I ummed and ahhed for months before investing in an expensive, high quality lunchbox. But it's honestly the best choice I made, and it's more than paid for itself by lasting for years. If you can afford it, I would recommend investing in a decent box that will last.

5. **Can your child open it independently?** This is more of an issue with younger children starting school or pre-school, but it's worth thinking through in advance. A box with a hinged lid and one flickable clip is much easier for small hands than a separate lid which needs lining up on the box to close (often with a decent amount of force) afterwards. Whichever lunchbox you decide on, be sure to practise this step at home a few times before starting school.

And whatever box you buy – name label it! After all your hard work finding a decent lunchbox to last, you don't want your child losing it in the first week of term and school not knowing who to return it to!

My Personal Favourite Lunchbox

After years of lunchbox packing and sharing packed lunches on Instagram, I have tried A LOT of lunchboxes. My go-to lunchboxes – and the ones that I use throughout this book – are the Yumbox range. They have lots of sections and a lid that seals each one of those sections individually, so you can pack wet foods next to crunchy foods and nothing will leak and nothing

 Original

 Panino

 Tapas

will go soft. You can even decant yoghurt from a family-sized tub directly into the box and it will stay put – no need for additional tubs.

Yumboxes come in three different sizes and layouts to best suit how your child likes to eat.

For primary school aged children

Yumbox Original: My personal favourite and the one we use nine times out of ten. It has six individual sections so is perfect for kids who like lots of variety at lunchtime.

Yumbox Panino: The same size as the original, but with only four sections: one large and three smaller ones, so it is perfect for children who eat a whole sandwich alongside a couple of other elements.

For bigger appetites

Yumbox Tapas: A bigger lunchbox aimed at older children, right through to adults (so they are perfect for work if you want to make a lunch for yourself while you're already making them for the kids). The tapas box comes with two different tray layouts so you can choose five or six sections depending on what you like to pack. The added bonus of the tapas design is that the trays are interchangeable – so you can have both trays to hand and simply use whichever suits what you're packing that day.

Top Tip!

If you have any questions about choosing a box, or would like my discount codes for Yumboxes, pop over to my Instagram page @thelunchbox.mama and drop me a message. I love a good chat!

And Another Excellent Option

If you can't justify spending this much on a lunchbox, then Sistema do a really good range of lunchboxes, often easily available in the supermarkets. Just be aware that although the box lid seals tightly to the box itself, the

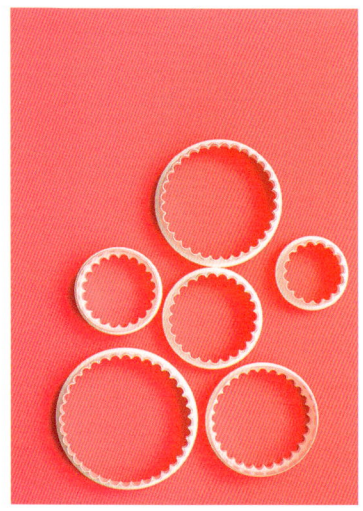

individual sections inside do not. Cut fruit, for example, will leak juice between sections, so you might need other tubs/packets as well.

Lunchbag

Once you have your lunchbox, you're going to want to protect it, and any food you pack in it, with an insulated lunchbag. This will help ensure food stays safe and cool until lunchtime. It will also help protect it from any accidental drops.

You'll also need some flat ice packs to pop in with the lunchbox to help keep the temperature of the food down; make sure you have enough to pop a couple in during the hotter weather in the weeks leading up to the summer holidays.

The Yumboxes fit in most rectangular lunchbags we've tried, mostly standard supermarket ones. I always let my children pick their lunchbag so that they are something they love. Throughout their school day, children are always being told what they have to do and when – so I like to let them have this moment in the middle of the day to have something really personal to them, which expresses their individual personality and reminds them of their life outside the classroom.

Top Tip!

Pop your packed lunchbox in the fridge until just before you leave the house – this helps ensure all food is as cool as possible when it goes into the lunchbag, rather than sitting out on the side for an hour first.

Cutters

Cutters are one of the easiest ways to make the food inside the lunchbox more attractive. They hardly add any extra prep time, and they really help lift a standard everyday lunch and turn it into something so much more fun!

Any of the above sets are a great place to start. Don't stress about having too many to begin with, they're fun to collect as you go – that way, your child(ren) will love each new idea as it

comes, rather than see all your ideas in the first week of term!

Type 'sandwich cutter' into any search engine and you'll get lots of options. But it's also worth keeping an eye out in kitchen shops (and even garden centres) for shaped cookie cutters. You will want to bear in mind the size of the sections of your lunchbox, and also that the cutter isn't too intricate. If it is, it'll leave you with a spindly sandwich and waste loads of bread – neither of which is quite the plan . . .

Top Tip!

If you're concerned about wasting bread when using cutters then flick through to page 63 for some ideas on using those extra bits up.

Top Tip!

If you don't have any cutters at home, and you want to check how they'd work for your family – go raid the kids' playdoh cutters – give them a really good wash and practise with those.

Food Picks

Food picks are great for children who are old enough to understand they are just for decoration and won't hurt themselves on them. Many packs say from age three onwards, but children will probably need to be a bit older to use them safely without your supervision. Food picks can easily add a pop of colour to a lunchbox or allow you to serve the same food but in a different, more interesting way. After spending time and money on selecting a BPA-free lunchbox, please make sure your picks are food safe too, especially if you're putting them directly into your children's food for a few hours (as this is where cheap plastic chemicals can leach into food).

Kitchen Essentials

Small sharp knife – my favourite is Victorinox Pointed Tip Paring Knife (8 cm). In pink, obviously! It's the perfect knife for fruit and veggies.

Decent kitchen scissors – my favourite are Fiskars – perfect for quickly cutting off crusts or slicing up pizza. Using scissors instead of a knife really is a kitchen gamechanger; try it if you haven't already.

Crinkle cutter, vegetable **peeler**, **cooling rack** and silicone **spatula**.

Silicone baking mats – these make life so much easier than spending time greasing trays, and nothing sticks to them. Give them a quick wipe afterwards and then chuck them on the top of everything in the top rack of your dishwasher; they'll soon be good to go again! OR you might like to try Scoville's Neverstick **baking trays**. I've recently discovered them and they are so good! Completely non-stick without needing greasing, and they go in the dishwasher afterwards too.

An airfryer – this is a big one, and not actually essential, but if you're considering getting one, I'm very happy for you to consider this your sign to go for it. It's so much quicker than heating up the oven, and so much more cost effective when you're only cooking a small amount for lunch.

Pick plates – the perfect sectioned plate for fussy easters who need something more grown up than the ones aimed at toddlers. They come in two sizes: a midi, which is the perfect size for a meal for one child, and a larger version called a biggie, which we love for sharing.

Serving board – a big round plate or wooden board is perfect. I have a personalised (gifted) one from a small business called Gifts in a Jiffy and it's the perfect size and great quality.

Nom Nom Kids – reusable snack bags and pouches. Bright, colourful, monster-themed pouches which you can fill and refill, rather than buying so many single-use plastic packed snacks. These also come in squeeze pouches for yogurts and jelly etc, which are super handy.

Optional Extras

- Silicone muffin cases in bright colours
- Dumpling makers
- Edible ink pens
- Sprinkles

Water Bottles

Not strictly lunchbox related, but a question I am asked a lot, as there is nothing more annoying than a water bottle that leaks over your child or their stuff every day. I asked my social media followers for their recommendations about four years ago and their overwhelming favourites were ion8 leakproof bottles. We've been using them ever since, and I recommend them to everyone now too. We love their stainless-steel insulated bottles which keep water fresh and cool all day at school, which I find helps kids to drink more too. They're also perfect for the adults in your family if a water bottle's something you like to use.

The Lunchbox Formula

So, we've got the basics sorted and your perfect lunchbox is sitting on the kitchen counter ready and waiting. The big question now is – how do you decide what to pack? It's time to introduce the Lunchbox Formula!

This simple formula that will enable you to take all the guesswork out of packing your lunchbox.

As adults, lots of us might think of lunch as a bit like a meal deal – a main with carbs, protein and salad, and a snack on the side. But when you have a fussy eater, especially one who doesn't like a lot of flavours mixed together, it's a concept that doesn't quite work. So, instead, aim to hit the five food groups (or as best your fussy eater will allow) in any way you can. You can even think of yourself as one of those fancy restaurant chefs who create versions of all the old classics – but deconstructed (it's all the same once it's inside their bellies). A lunchbox with five or more separate sections is perfect for this as you can add some bread in one section, some protein in another and anything salady that your child does like in another.

In every lunch you pack, aim to hit these five food groups, and then you've done your best to send your child to school with a balanced lunch.

Five Food Groups

Grains/Carbs
+
Protein
+
Dairy
(or calcium rich alternative)
+
Fruit
+
Vegetable

Building a Lunchbox

Sometimes the mental load can feel like the hardest thing about packing lunches. Once all the necessary food is in the house, it's much easier to pack healthy, balanced lunches, but what about the days or weeks where you just don't know what to buy, or where to start?

Two Cheat Sheets

Here, I've set out two cheat sheets which I hope will help relieve a little pressure from your amazing, but constantly spinning, mum-brain. One is store cupboard essentials. I recommend trying to always have a selection of these in the house, so you've always got something to create a packed lunch with even if you haven't done a proper shop in a while.

The other is the fussy eater cheat sheet. This is a list of potential fruits and vegetables you COULD buy, and some tick boxes so you can chart which child eats what. The aim here is to make your weekly food shop just a little bit easier. Hopefully, it will also help you mix up a bit of variety, without wasting foods you'd forgotten they don't like.

Cheat Sheet No. 1
Store Cupboard Essentials

I don't have all of these in all the time, but if you have a selection from each group on hand there will always be *something* to make for lunches. If you're feeling stuck in a boring lunch rut, come back and scan this list and the following cheat sheets, to help inspire you to mix things up a bit. You might also share some of these ideas with your fussy eater to see what they like the sound of – and that can help get you out of the rut too.

Snack Cupboard	Fridge	Freezer	Baking
• Breadsticks • Crackers • Rice crackers • Oatcakes • Pretzels • Pretzel sticks • Veggie straws • Low sugar breakfast cereals • Dried fruits • Fruit snacks • Jelly • Biscuits	• Cheese • Yoghurt • Eggs • Meats/alternatives • Butter/spreadable butter • Puff pastry (ready rolled) • Fruit • Vegetables • Picnic foods like cocktail sausages, mini scotch eggs, sausage rolls	• Bread for sandwiches • Leftover wraps, pittas, naan breads, etc • Picnic foods like cocktail sausages, mini scotch eggs, sausage rolls • Cheese scones – see page 81	• Plain flour • Spelt flour (to replace plain flour in any recipe for a less processed version) • Self-raising flour • Oats (can be ground to make oat flour) • Baking powder • Vanilla extract • Granulated sugar • Sprinkles • Edible ink pens • Icing sugar • Edible eyes • Food colouring

Cheat Sheet No. 2

The Fussy Eater Cheat Sheet

Top Tip!

Use the tick boxes to help track who likes what, to make the food shop a touch easier. I suggest ticking the boxes in pencil, because we all know how kids like to change their minds on these things!

Grains & Carbs

- Bread
  - *Wholemeal*
  - *White*
  - *50/50*
  - *Seeded*
- Bagels
- Bread rolls
- Breadsticks
- Breakfast cereals
- Cereal bar
- Chapati
- Corn cakes
- Chickpea crisps
- Croissants
- Crumpets
- Crackers
- English muffins
  - *White*
  - *Wholemeal*
- Flatbreads
- Fruit loaf
- Hot cross buns
- Lentil crisps
- Naan bread
- Oats
- Oat bars
- Porridge flapjacks (see page 77)
- Pancakes (see page 72)
- Part-baked rolls
- Pasta
- Popping corn/plain popcorn*
- Puff pastry (ready rolled)
- Pitta bread
- Pizza dough
- Puff pastry
- Rice cakes
  - *Plain*
  - *Flavoured*
- Savoury muffins
- Teacakes
- Veggie sticks
- Waffles
- Wraps
  - *Wholemeal*
  - *White*
  - *Seeded*

THE FUSSY EATER CHEAT SHEET   17

Cheat Sheet No. 2
The Fussy Eater Cheat Sheet

Proteins & Dairy

- Beef
- Bacon – smoked
- Bacon – unsmoked
- Beans
- Cheese
  - *Mild Cheddar*
  - *Mature Cheddar*
  - *Double Gloucester*
  - *Edam*
  - *Cheese spread*
  - *Cream cheese*
  - *Cottage cheese*
  - *Mozzarella*
- Chicken
  - *Nuggets*
  - *Roast*
  - *Sliced sandwich meat*
- Chickpeas
- Chorizo – sliced sandwich meat
- Cooking chorizo (fried)
- Eggs
  - *Hard-boiled*
  - *Egg mayo (or softer boiled and mashed without mayo)*
  - *OR: eggs in baked goods*
- Fish
  - *Tinned*
  - *Smoked salmon*
- Flaxseed
- Fromage frais
  - *Kids' pots*
  - *Plain*
  - *Plain with jam added*
- Hummus
- Leftover meatballs
- Nut butters (not for school)
  - *Peanut*
  - *Almond*
  - *Cashew*
  - *Nuts (not for school)**
- Pepperoni
- Prawns
- Salami
- Sausages
- Seeds
- Seed butter
- Turkey
- Yoghurt
  - *Greek*
  - *Kefir*
  - *Dairy free*

Cheat Sheet No. 2

The Fussy Eater Cheat Sheet

Fruit

- Apples**
  - *Green* ☐ ☐ ☐
  - *Red* ☐ ☐ ☐
  - *Dried apple rings* ☐ ☐ ☐
- Apricots
  - *Fresh* ☐ ☐ ☐
  - *Dried* ☐ ☐ ☐
- Avocado (or guacamole) ☐ ☐ ☐
- Banana ☐ ☐ ☐
- Banana chips ☐ ☐ ☐
- Blackberries ☐ ☐ ☐
- Cherries (destoned)* ☐ ☐ ☐
- Cranberries ☐ ☐ ☐
- Dates (destoned) ☐ ☐ ☐
- Figs
  - *Fresh* ☐ ☐ ☐
  - *Dried* ☐ ☐ ☐
- Freeze dried fruits ☐ ☐ ☐
- Fruit pouches ☐ ☐ ☐
- Grapes
  - *Green** ☐ ☐ ☐
  - *Red** ☐ ☐ ☐
  - *Black** ☐ ☐ ☐
- Goji berries ☐ ☐ ☐
- Kiwi ☐ ☐ ☐
- Mango
  - *Fresh* ☐ ☐ ☐
  - *Dried* ☐ ☐ ☐
- Melon
  - *Cantaloupe* ☐ ☐ ☐
  - *Honeydew* ☐ ☐ ☐
  - *Watermelon* ☐ ☐ ☐
- Nectarines ☐ ☐ ☐
- Oranges
  - *Small/easy peeler* ☐ ☐ ☐
  - *Large/Jaffa* ☐ ☐ ☐
- Olives* ☐ ☐ ☐
- Passion fruit ☐ ☐ ☐
- Peach ☐ ☐ ☐
- Pineapple
  - *Fresh* ☐ ☐ ☐
  - *Dried* ☐ ☐ ☐
- Plum ☐ ☐ ☐
- Pomegranate ☐ ☐ ☐
- Prune ☐ ☐ ☐
- Raspberries ☐ ☐ ☐
- Raisins ☐ ☐ ☐
- Strawberries
  - *Fresh* ☐ ☐ ☐
  - *Freeze-dried* ☐ ☐ ☐
- Sultanas ☐ ☐ ☐

Cheat Sheet No. 2

The Fussy Eater Cheat Sheet

Vegetables

- Broccoli ☐ ☐ ☐
- Cauliflower ☐ ☐ ☐
- Celery ☐ ☐ ☐
- Carrots
  - *Non-organic* ☐ ☐ ☐
  - *Organic (if your kids don't like that soapy aftertaste of carrots, then it's worth trying organic!)* ☐ ☐ ☐
  - *Baby* ☐ ☐ ☐
- Corn on the cob ☐ ☐ ☐
- Cucumber
  - *Normal sized* ☐ ☐ ☐
  - *Mini* ☐ ☐ ☐
- Edamame ☐ ☐ ☐

- Iceberg lettuce ☐ ☐ ☐
- Mushrooms ☐ ☐ ☐
- Olives* ☐ ☐ ☐
- Peppers (including minis)
  - *Red* ☐ ☐ ☐
  - *Orange* ☐ ☐ ☐
  - *Yellow* ☐ ☐ ☐
  - *Green* ☐ ☐ ☐
- Seaweed snacks ☐ ☐ ☐
- Spinach ☐ ☐ ☐
- Sugar snap peas ☐ ☐ ☐
- Tomatoes
  - *Salad/large* ☐ ☐ ☐
  - *Cherry** ☐ ☐ ☐
  - *Plum** ☐ ☐ ☐

* A Note On Choking Hazards

Please be aware of potential choking hazards for any children six or younger, and if you're in any doubt about a particular food, I would always recommend cutting it up. For me, school isn't the place to take the risk and it's better to learn to manage those trickier foods under close supervision rather than when chatting and giggling with their friends and not necessarily paying so much attention to what they're eating.

** No more brown apples!

Many children will turn their noses up at sliced apple that's beginning to go brown, and while slightly browned slices are safe to eat, I would never convince my children to do so! I find a few things help. Get your apple slices in an airtight container sharpish so they can't react with the air and brown. If that's enough, then perfect, but if not you can briefly soak your apple slices in water for 3 to 5 minutes then either shake or pat them dry before packing. Even better than this, a pinch of salt in the water before soaking is an effective way to stop the dreaded browning.

So, What's Next?

Now that you have a house full of foods you could pack for lunch, you'll either feel relieved that you can just grab and go each morning (or night before). Or you'll be spurred on to plan which days you'll pack what. There's no right or wrong at this point, it just depends how you like to do life.

For the planners among us I have these two printables you can use to plan the foods you're going to pack either in a list form or in a lunchbox visual. I find the mini lunchbox diagrams a great way to get the kids involved in the packing. They love to sit with a sheet and fill in some ideas for the week ahead. You can find both of these printables via this QR code, so you can print as many copies as you need, or print one and laminate it and use it with whiteboard pens.

Scan me!

Scan this QR code or type the URL below into your browser.

https://blackandwhitepublishing.com/pages/the-lunchbox-mama

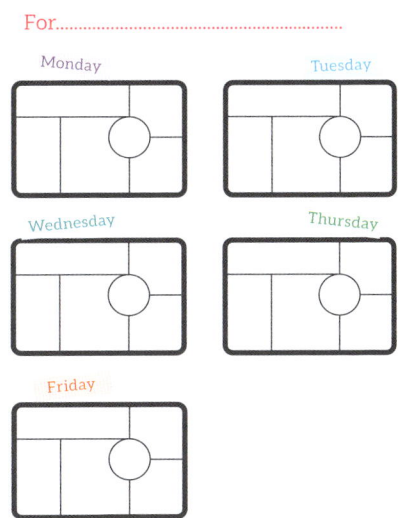

The Lunchboxes

Easy Wins
Starting the Week Strong
End of the Week
Themed Lunches
School Holiday Lunches
Fun at Home

Easy Wins

Any win, however small, is always a win – especially when it comes to fussy eating. Making small changes that encourage your child to try something they'd usually outright reject is huge!

There can be so much anxiety that gets in the way of a fussy eater trying something new, that they immediately say no before even thinking about it. But, by making it feel more like fun, drawing their interest and presenting it differently you can open the conversation and gradually bring them round to the idea of at least trying it.

These easy wins can work really well on a child's favourite foods – I find that by presenting them in lots of different ways this helps children not get stuck on an expectation that, for example, cucumbers are always cut in sticks. As we all know, this can then lead children to believe that they only like cucumbers cut in sticks and will refuse them in slices!

So, let's have some fun!

Cucumber Crowns

Like plenty of children, cucumber is the one and only vegetable my daughter ate for a long time. But it became repetitive and boring for her, eating the same slices or sticks every day, so we like to mix it up as much as possible – which has the added bonus of making it a little less mind numbing for me! Normally, when children are served cucumbers, they are mostly cut in sticks or circles, but it's great to mix this up and serve them in as many different ways as possible, so they don't get stuck thinking that they only like cucumber a certain way.

Fussy Eater Tip

Help your child feel involved in their food choices and use the image below so they can choose how they'd like their cucumbers cut. (Some days, not every day!) Giving them as much control as possible, over the things you're happy for them to have control over, makes them more likely to co-operate with the things you need them to co-operate with!

My everyday faithfuls are . . .

Then . . . on the days you're feeling a little extra: make like a queen and cut crowns!

You'll need

- Cucumber
- A paring knife (a small sharp knife with a sharp point and a blade only about 1 cm long – my favourite is recommended on page 12)

What to do

Cut a chunk of cucumber about the depth of your lunchbox. It's important to check so you know it will fit in once prepared.

Next, cut a small zigzag line around the middle of your cucumber chunk. Picture the spikes of a crown and start by poking the knife in at an angle (on the wonk one way) through the skin and into the middle(ish) of the cucumber.

Remove the knife and line it up at an opposite angle (on the wonk the other way) and cut into the centre again.

Keep going all the way around the cucumber and then pull the halves apart.

TA-DAH!

If you're finding the cucumber won't pull apart, just check all your zigzag cuts are fully joined up, then try again.

CROWNS ALL ROUND

Once you've perfected this cutting technique, you can use it on other fruits, like kiwis (if you eat the skin), oranges, cherry tomatoes, grapes and even blueberries (for older children who don't need them cut in half lengthways to avoid choking). It does work on other vegetables like carrots, but because they're much denser carving out those crowns is a lot more like hard work!

Love Heart Strawberries

Nothing looks cuter than a little bit of extra love in their lunchbox! This is SUPER easy. Just two cuts with a knife and BAM you're an instant fun mum!

You'll need

- Strawberries
- A small sharp knife

What to do

Grab your strawberries, wash them and pat dry as normal.

Now instead of just lopping the leafy bit off with a flat cut, you're going to cut a V shape.

Grab the leaves and twist to get rid of most of the foliage. Now you can see what you're doing.

On one side of the stalk cut at an angle down and towards the middle of the strawberry – just about 1 cm as shown.

Then match the other side to create a V shape.

Slide the stalk out and ta-dah! Love heart strawberry! You can either leave them whole or cut in half – just cut across the bumps as shown. And not in the middle of the V you just created! I learned this lesson the hard way . . .

Veggie Cutters

If knife skills aren't for you, then a set of vegetable cutters might be the answer. These are extra strong mini cutters that come in a variety of shapes, perfect for cutting through tougher veggies like carrots and peppers.

You can either cut out some shapes and pack the cutout and the outer, so there's no additional waste, but it's so much more fun to eat!

Or, if your fussy eater doesn't mind different foods touching, make lunches super colourful with some veggie swapsies like the ones shown here.

Fussy eater tip

If your child doesn't yet like foods touching, then you can try this. Cut the different food options and pack them in separate sections, and drop a vague comment about how they could try mixing the colours up themselves, if they wanted. You might find they are more likely to do it themselves than accept it already mixed. Equally it may just be a flat 'no' for now – that's absolutely okay too.

A note on the word 'yet'

Note the 'yet'. I find it really helps to include 'yet' when talking to my children about what they don't like. It helps gently reinforce the idea that we need to try foods a few times before we decide if we really don't like them, and that our tastes can change over time.

Heart Cocktail Sausages & Mini Carrots

This trick works with any small cylindrical foods, from cocktail sausages, mini carrots or even a little plum tomato. These are better suited to older kids who won't hurt themselves on a food pick at school – and would also need to be cut in half lengthways, before transforming, for those young enough that they might be a choking hazard.

You'll need

- Your chosen cylindrical food
- A sharp knife
- A cocktail stick or reusable food pick

What to do

Make a diagonal cut across the middle of the sausage, like this:

Then flip one half over to create your heart shape and secure with your food pick.

Step 1: Cut

Step 2: Flip one half over

Step 3: Lift both ends upwards

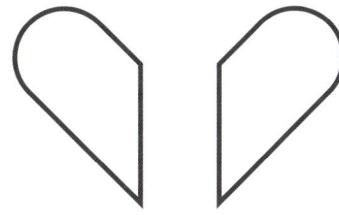

Step 4: Bring together to create your heart shape

Food Picks

> **Top Tip!**
> Add instant drama by creating mini kebabs with fruit, veggies and mini sandwich stacks and pancakes. We love fruit with eyes, too! See photos of food pick ideas on page 11.

Food picks are a great way to add a little more fun to a lunchbox, with minimal effort. Hurrah!

They're also perfect if your child doesn't love getting their fingers messy when eating – they can use them like a tiny fork, which is great for those fine motor skills too. Just be aware of any minimum ages on the picks you choose and talk to your child first about ensuring they keep them in their lunchbox after they've eaten. (And not to take them out onto the playground to be used as tiny swords – no, I'm absolutely not speaking from personal experience, obviously!)

Spotty Dino Eggs

Hard-boiled eggs are a great source of protein to keep your child full for an afternoon of learning. But they're not always the most 'fun' food. And they can be stinky – so if you think that might bother your child at school, you can always serve these alongside breakfast or dinner at home instead.

You'll need

- Hard-boiled eggs
- Edible ink pens

What to do

Gently crack your cooled, boiled egg and remove all the shell.

Make sure your egg is nice and dry (if you've washed the last of the shell crumbs away), then use edible ink pens to draw little spots on the eggs.

These are perfect alongside dinosaur-shaped sandwiches if you want to tie the theme together. You can take it a step further and include:

- dino footprints – cut from cucumbers
- dino teeth – light coloured cheese cut into tall triangles
- dino bones – stick-shaped snacks (pretzel sticks, twig-like crisps)
- chicken (or veggie/vegan equivalent) dinosaur nuggets
- dinosaur-shaped cereal
- raw broccoli as tiny trees (if your child would be happy to try!)

> **Top Tip!**
> At Easter, draw squiggly patterns or springtime decorations on your hard-boiled eggs.

Heart Eggs

You'll need

- 1 hard-boiled egg
- A long piece of card (about 15 cm long, by 10 cm wide) folded in half in a long, narrow V shape
- A piece of tin foil
- 1 chopstick
- 2 elastic bands

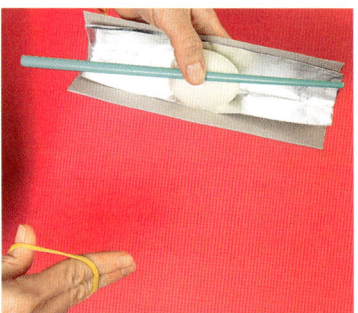

What to do

Take a cooled, peeled hard-boiled egg.

Place your tin foil flat inside the V-shaped cardboard and lay the egg down in the middle.

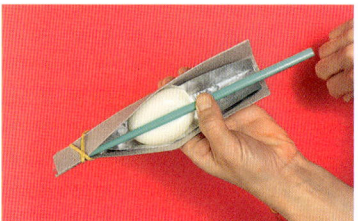

Holding onto the egg and cardboard (I know it's very slippery!), carefully place the chopstick on top of the egg. Make sure it's over the middle of the egg as this is going to be the dip in the top of your heart.

Take an elastic band and pop it around the card and chopstick at each end (not touching your egg). Make sure the elastic band is tight enough that the chopstick is pulled down, squashing the top of the egg.

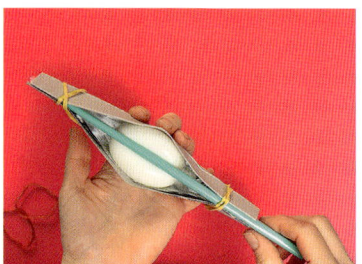

Leave for at least 20 minutes to set the shape. If you're making these the night before, you can pop the whole contraption into an airtight box in the fridge overnight.

Undo your elastic bands and take out your egg. Use a sharp knife to cut it in half across the bumps and pull apart to reveal two rather lovely heart-shaped eggs!

DIY Dippers

Bento boxes are perfect to help reduce single-use plastic waste with dipping snacks like this. Kids love those cheese spread dipping snacks you can buy pre-made, and while these are great when you need to grab them out and about, you'll save so much money making them yourself, when you can.

All you need is one snack from each of these tables and you're set. This is a brilliant activity to get your child involved in at the weekend and choose which dip and dippers you're going to buy this week. This helps your mental load by not making you responsible for every decision all the time, and helps children to learn to make decisions for themselves too. You can even get them helping to pack their chosen dips and dippers into their lunchbox (while you do any of the other million jobs on the to-do list in your head).

Dips

Cheese spread	Hummus
Chocolate spread*	Nut butter*
Cream cheese	Salsa
Dips (shop bought or homemade)	Sandwich filler with small pieces
Egg mayo	Seed butter*
Guacamole	

* Depending on where you're planning to enjoy your dippers (be aware of nut-free schools).

Dippers

Breadsticks	Peppers, sliced
Carrot sticks	Pretzel sticks
Celery	Tortilla chips
Cucumber sticks	Veggie straws
Homemade nachos (see page 75)	Wholegrain crisps
Mini crackers	

Jelly in the Box

Jelly isn't the most obvious lunchbox food, unless you're buying those pre-made individual tubs, which are both much more expensive than making your own, and also cause unnecessary plastic waste. But making your own is SO EASY and my kids LOVE it!

Make up your jelly as per the packet instructions, then pour directly into the Yumbox tray and leave it in the fridge overnight. In the morning, the jelly should be safely set and ready for you to pack the rest of the lunch around it. Please do not try this in a box that does not seal each section individually, or you will have a very sad kid come lunchtime!

Jelly is also great in a pouch, either in the lunch bag next to your bento box, or as a snack on the way home from school. We love the Nom Nom Kids reusable pouches for after school jelly.

Add extra goodness

I see lots of people adding pieces of fruit to their children's jelly – and this is a great idea if your children will eat it. BUT do not feel bad if you know your kid would outright reject their jelly if it had chunks of fruit in. For example, I know my kids would not eat strawberry jelly with strawberries in, but they would one hundred per cent eat the jelly with the strawberries on the side. So, it's a no brainer – that's what we do. After all, it's all the same once it's in their bellies!

One goodness hack I do like is to add some fruit juice (of a fruit they'd be less likely to eat) to the jelly mix, to add some additional nutrients that way. Why not try adding up to 200ml pineapple juice to your next batch of jelly and see if the kids notice?

Fussy eater tip

Start small and build it up. Add a splash of the less familiar juice the first time and gradually increase up to about 200ml.

Top Tip!

For lunchbox jelly, make it with slightly less water than the instructions suggest, to keep it a little firmer than normal (especially when the weather is hot). And for pouches, use a little extra water to make it softer and easier to suck out of the pouch. Equally, I don't always do this with pouches, as it keeps them beautifully quiet on the walk home; it takes them ages to eat and no one can argue while they're eating jelly out of a pouch!

Sandwich Pockets

These cute pockets are perfect if you're keen to try some new ideas, but don't have any cutters yet. They seal a small sandwich all around the edge, so they're perfect little crust-free and soft sandwich pockets. If you're having them at home, you can pop them in the airfryer to make a warm toastie version. If you don't have an airfryer you can pop them in the toaster in a toaster bag.

You'll need

- 2 slices of bread
- Your choice of filling: a soft spread like cream cheese, jam, grated cheese or sandwich meat
- A strong pint glass

What to do

Lay out your 2 slices of bread on a chopping board.

Add your filling into the centre of one slice of bread, in an approximate circle shape just a little smaller than the width of the top of your pint glass.

Lay the other slice of bread on top to form a sandwich.

Place your pint glass upside down, over the top of the filling bump, and carefully press down, rocking the edge of the glass in a circular motion to help it cut through the bread. Once the glass is nearly through, press it down and twist clockwise and anti-clockwise to ensure you've got a nice neat cut.

If your sandwich pocket comes up inside the glass, gently poke one side to allow it to fall out.

You can make these pockets in a variety of different sizes with any glasses you have in the cupboard. Just double check the top of the glass will fit in the lunchbox you plan to pack the pockets in, before you begin.

Chocolate Spread Hack

In lunches, as in life, we sometimes have to work with what we've got! And if you've got fussy eaters, there can be a lot of mum guilt from comparing what pre-kids you thought you'd feed your kids, versus what they actually eat once they are real little people. I'm a firm believer that with time, encouragement and exposure, our fussy eaters will begin to broaden their horizons. (Things might be different for those children with unique difficulties and/or neurodiversities.) But in the meantime, they still need to be fed. So, if like me, you're in a phase that requires chocolate spread or jam sandwiches, that you wish could be made just a teeny bit healthier – then here's a hack!

You'll need

- 1 or 2 slices of bread (I love the 50/50 ones that look white but have some of the goodness of wholemeal)
- Chocolate spread or jam (ensure chocolate spread is nut free for school)
- Ground flaxseed*

What to do

Add your sandwich filler to one side of the bread, then sprinkle over a pinch of ground flaxseed. Use the tip of your knife to swish over the flaxseed and mix it into the sandwich filler (so no eagle eyes will detect any difference).

Continue to make your sandwich and pack as usual.

Top Tip!

* You can buy ground flaxseed, sometimes called milled flaxseed, in the supermarket alongside all the other seeds. Don't bother with whole flaxseeds, as they are much harder to digest so your fussy eater won't get all the benefits. Ground seeds are also less detectable, so you have more chance of sneaking some goodness in, undiscovered. Once your children are old enough not to outright reject anything new, you can have a chat about why these are super-sprinkles and offer them as toast toppings and on porridge, giving them the control and opportunity to make health-boosting decisions for their own bodies

Pepperoni Roses

These look super fancy, but they are honestly super easy and will elevate your lunchbox game with minimal effort.

You'll need

- 4 to 6 circular slices of pepperoni, salami or similar (you can make this work with ham if that's better for your child, but you'll need to cut the ham into 4 to 6 cm circles with a cookie cutter first).

What to do

Lay one circular slice on a board, then lay the next one on top about halfway along. Continue adding the rest of your slices, like this.

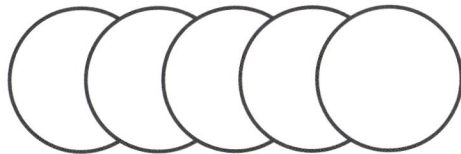

Fold the bottom halves of your meat up towards the top, so you have a long line of semicircles all attached together.

Turn your chopping board 90 degrees and tightly roll from bottom up to the top.

Secure the rose by popping it in a small section of the lunchbox or by poking a pick stick (or cocktail stick) through near the base to hold it together.

Five Food Groups

Grains/Carbs

+

Protein

+

Dairy
(or calcium rich alternative)

+

Fruit

+

Vegetable

Starting the Week Strong

Lunches from Monday to Wednesday

You've done the shopping, you've got fresh bread and lunch options in the fridge, and you're ready to get packing.

To keep these lunches fussy eater friendly, I'm showing you each idea, which can be made in a variety of flavours, so you can pick what would work best for your child. Also, because I am aware that a lot of fussy eaters tend not to like too many foods and flavours mixed, these ideas are the main element – you can think of them as 'the star of the show' – and then using the Lunchbox Formula explained in the introduction, you will just need to add the additional food groups.

So, if you make one of these sandwich alternatives which uses carbs and protein, you'll need to add some dairy (or alternative), plus fruit and vegetables. Whereas if your fussy eater prefers their carbs and protein separately, and you make an idea using a non-protein-rich sandwich filling, try and pop a separate protein hit into their lunch as an extra.

Sandwich Roll-Ups

You'll need

- 1 slice of bread
- A flat/thinly spreadable sandwich filler, like cheese spread or jam (see the box for more options)

What to do

Remove crusts if needed (feel free to keep them on if everyone will be happy) and roll the bread flat with a rolling pin.*

Add your filling in a thin layer all over.

From the bottom, tightly roll the bread all the way to the top turning it into a swirly sausage.

Slice into thin (about 1 cm) swirls for younger kids, or keep as bigger chunks or even one long sausage shape for older kids.

Depending on the roll-up filling you've chosen, you will have ticked grains, and possibly dairy or protein, off your lunchbox formula. Check the checklist and add anything else you need.

*If you haven't got a rolling pin, save an old glass bottle, remove the label and give it a good clean in hot soapy water – hey presto, one DIY rolling pin!

Lunchbox Formula Checklist

- Grains/Carbs ✓
- +
- Protein ☐
- +
- Dairy ☐
- +
- Fruit ☐
- +
- Vegetable ☐

More sandwich filler ideas

- Cream cheese and jam (call them cheesecake swirls, if this helps)
- Cheese spread (with or without some added finely grated cheese for extra goodness)
- Pumpkin seed/granola butter and jam (nut-free peanut butter and jam vibes!)
- Jam or chocolate spread, with added hidden flaxseed (see page 39)
- Hummus
- Sandwich meat
- Thinly sliced or grated cheese
- Egg mayo

Peek-a-Boo Sandwiches

Lunchbox Formula Checklist

Grains/Carbs ✓
+
Protein ☐
+
Dairy ☐
+
Fruit ☐
+
Vegetable ☐

These are perfect for kids who will happily eat a proper sandwich, just way cuter! But they are also great for previous sandwich refusers, or those who are just beginning to make their way through a proper sandwich. The little cutouts look super cute and way more enticing than a standard slab of sandwich.

Equally, if you look at these and think 'what's the point' then consider your kid already a good sandwich eater, and flick on for more ideas.

You'll need

- 1 or 2 slices of bread (depending on your child's appetite)
- Your chosen sandwich filler – something a different, brighter colour to the bread works best
- A small veggie cutter – see page 29 for ideas

What to do

Remove bread crusts (if needed).

ONE SLICE OF BREAD
Cut your bread in half and add the filling to one half.

Cut the other half in half again.

Use your cutter to remove a shape from the centre of each of those two quarters.

Place these two quarters on top of your sandwich filler to make your sandwich.

Cut through the already cut centre line to make two mini sandwiches.

TWO SLICES OF BREAD
Add your sandwich filling on top of one slice of bread.

Grab the other slice of bread and cut it into quarters.

Using your shape cutter, cut shapes from the middle of two of the quarters.

Place all four quarters on top of your sandwich filler to make your sandwich.

Then, following your already cut quarter-lines, cut down through the rest of the sandwich.

Place the two normal sandwiches at the bottom of the lunchbox, and stack the peek-a-boo ones on top.

With that done . . . Carbs are definitely ticked off from the checklist. And, depending on your sandwich filler, you might have added protein or dairy too. Pop in some fruit and veg, and anything else you need.

Shape Cutters

Sometimes the easiest way to add variety to a fussy eater's lunch is to grab a cookie cutter – and change the shape of their favourite sandwich. You make their safe, usual lunch look like something new and different, but you know when they eat it, it will taste just as they expect. This works as positive reinforcement for your fussy eater. They can think, 'Okay, I tried something new today, and it was okay. I liked it.' And while it's not really new, it can help massively to have a few of these positive experiences, rather than them being brave and trying a new sandwich filler and not liking it, which then proves to them that it wasn't worth trying.

You'll need

- Your usual sandwich
- A cutter

What to do

Experiment with bigger and smaller cutters and see what your child eats best. Some kids might prefer one bigger proper sandwich, whereas others find it less intimidating to have a few small ones they can easily pick up and graze on.

You can also turn these into full themed lunchboxes – see the Themed Lunches chapter for more ideas.

Depending on your child's favourite sandwich, tick off the food groups already packed, and add the others to their lunchbox as tasty extras.

Lunchbox Formula Checklist

- Grains/Carbs ✓
- \+
- Protein ☐
- \+
- Dairy ☐
- \+
- Fruit ☐
- \+
- Vegetable ☐

Sausage Roll-Ups

Lunchbox Formula Checklist
Grains/Carbs ✓
+
Protein ✓
+
Dairy ☐
+
Fruit ☐
+
Vegetable ☐

Perfect with leftover sausages (if you have more self-control than my family!), or precooked cocktail sausages from the supermarket. Remember that sausages can be a choking hazard for younger children, so if in doubt, slice any sausages lengthways before rolling in bread – they look the same but are safer, especially at school when they're eating while chatting or laughing with their friends.

You'll need

- 1 or 2 slices of bread
- Cooked and cooled sausages (fat ones, chipolatas, veggie sausages, whatever you like)

What to do

Remove crusts from the bread (if needed).

IF USING LEFTOVER SAUSAGES
Place one sausage* at the bottom of the bread slice and tightly roll them together all the way up.

Either keep whole and secure with a food pick, or cut into smaller chunks or slices, as pictured.

IF USING COCKTAIL SAUSAGES
Cut your bread into thirds – crustless works best here – cutting from top to bottom (not side to side), giving you three long strips.

Pop one sausage* at the bottom of each strip and roll up! Secure with a food pick.

Sausages and bread will tick off the carbs and protein from your checklist. Hit the other three food groups and you're all set.

* Sliced lengthways if needed, and then popped back together.

Top Tip!
Cocktail sausages are often safe for home freezing, so buy a big pack when they're on offer, keep some in the fridge for the next couple of days and pop the rest in the freezer to have on hand when you run out of fresh things to pack.

Sandwich Kebabs

Perfect if your child likes small bites, but also great if they like some variety – by which I mean they seem to get bored eating a whole sandwich that tastes the same . . .

You'll need

- 2 slices of bread
- Your chosen sandwich fillers (but nothing messy for this one – things like ham or spreads work best)
- Some mini sticks like these pick sticks, or cocktail sticks if not.

What to do

Remove the crusts and make your sandwich as normal.

Cut into thirds one way.

Then again into thirds (or quarters) the other way, making 9 or 12 mini sandwich bites.

Pop three sandwiches on a stick, in a little stack.

> **Top Tip!**
> If you want to do multiple sandwich flavours, remove the crusts and chop your bread into thirds straight away. Add a different filling to each third, and add another third to make your sandwich before chopping them into little bite-sized pieces and stacking. Stack all the same on each stick, or mix it up.

You'll have packed carbs and possibly dairy or protein by now, so grab some fruit and veg and anything else you need, and you've completed the checklist!

Lunchbox Formula Checklist

Grains/Carbs ✓
+
Protein ☐
+
Dairy ☐
+
Fruit ☐
+
Vegetable ☐

Sandwich Sunshines

Sandwiches with certain fillings can be a pain for younger children who pick one up only to let all the filling fall promptly out the back . . .

Enter the sandwich sunshine! Made with little dumpling makers and a circle of sliced bread, these dumpling makers seal around the edge so nothing gets dropped by tiny hands fumbling to pick a sandwich up while chatting to friends and being distracted by everything that's going on in the dinner hall.

They're also perfect for adding a new-ish sandwich filling (those ones you KNOW they would like if they would just try) – pop it inside the sandwich sunshine, and that way they won't be put off by the visual of a new filler staring them in the face.

I would recommend talking about what's in the sandwich before school – no fussy eater I know would try a random sandwich with no idea what's inside! I've found this helps encourage your child to get over the hurdle of being put off a new food simply because it looks different. As an example, my son used to eat roast chicken and I wanted to introduce the idea of chicken mayo, but he wasn't keen to try. I knew if I sent it as a normal sandwich, he would see the mayonnaise and be put off. But by sealing it up in a 'sunshine', which he already liked and was familiar with, he tried and – lo and behold! – he liked it.

You'll need

- Dumpling makers
- A cookie cutter if you have one (if not a sturdy glass or mug with an opening the same size, or slightly bigger than your dumpling maker, when it's laid out flat)
- 1 or 2 slices of bread (1 per dumpling)
- Sandwich fillers – pretty much anything cut small works here

What to do

Cut out a circle from each slice of bread. Use a circular cookie cutter if you have one.

Now place the bread circle on the top of the dumpling maker and add a little sandwich filler to the centre of the bread (leave the edge bare all the way around like a pizza crust so it will seal together).

Fold the dumpling maker in half and press the sides together firmly to seal the bread. Carefully remove and trim any excess, and ta-dah! A tiny, beautiful sandwich sunshine!

Repeat as many times as needed – and save those bread offcuts in a tub. See page 63 for ideas on how to use them up.

You'll have packed your carbs and possibly either protein and/or dairy in your sunshines, so add some fruit, veg and tasty extras, and you're set.

Cold Toasties

If a toastie isn't toastie, is it still a toastie!? Ah, that eternal question . . .

But if a fussy eater likes it, even if it sounds a bit weird, is it still a winner? ABSOLUTELY!

You can use a sandwich toaster if you have one, and if the finished toastie will fit in your lunchbox, but if you need a frying pan option, this is how we make them.

You'll need

- 2 slices of bread
- Cheeeeeeese
- Any extras your fussy eater likes, like ham, tomato, pepper, chopped up small (no raw meats, please)
- A frying pan
- A wire cooling rack

What to do

Heat a frying pan (big enough to fit the bread in) on a medium to high heat.

Butter one slice of bread and place butter side down in the pan.

Add cheese and any extra fillings on top of the bread.

Butter the other slice of bread and place it, butter side up, on top of your fillings.

Lunchbox Formula Checklist

Grains/Carbs ✓
+
Protein ✓
+
Dairy ✓
+
Fruit ☐
+
Vegetable ☐

Top Tip!

You can mix up the presentation by making a stripy toastie in a panini/grilling machine or even make a waffled toastie in a waffle maker. I find that waffle ones can get a bit stuck, so be sure to oil your waffle maker before you add your buttered bread.

After a couple of minutes, use a spatula to peek under the bottom slice of bread and see if it's browning. Once lightly toasted all over, flip the whole sandwich over.

Cook the other side for a couple of minutes, until lightly brown all over.

Remove the toastie from the pan and place on a cooling rack to cool – if you place it on a flat surface, it will go all sweaty and soggy, and no one wants that!

Once fully cooled, chop to fit into your lunchbox.

You'll have packed carbs and probably dairy or protein by now, so grab some fruit and veg and anything else you need, and you've completed the checklist!

Omelette Wraps

Eggs are brilliant for kids. They contain high quality protein, iron, fats and vitamins. But if your child doesn't love the idea of a hard-boiled egg, then it can be tricky to find a way to pack them for lunch. Enter the omelette wrap!

You'll need

- A tortilla wrap around the same size as your best non-stick frying pan. If you only have a smaller frying pan, go for mini wraps, but if you have a big pan, you'll need big wraps!
- An egg or two (depending on whether you went big or small above)
- Tasty extras such as cheese, tomato, peppers and ham (be sure to cook any raw meats first)
- A knob of butter
- A non-stick frying pan, with a lid if you have one, or a spare baking sheet works if not
- A cooling rack

What to do

Crack your egg into a small bowl and beat.

Chop up any tasty extras into small pieces, and grate any cheese.

Add your chosen tasty extras to the beaten egg and mix together.

Heat your frying pan on a medium heat for a minute or so until heated through.

Add a little butter to the pan, and once melted, tip in the egg mixture. Tilt the pan so the egg mixture spreads out all over the base.

Cook until the egg is set on the bottom, but is still a little wet and runny on top, then lay the wrap carefully on top of the omelette, and gently press it down with a spatula.

Put the lid on the pan and cook for one minute, until the wrap is warmed and the egg set.

Flip your creation onto a chopping board (wrap side down), and once cool enough to handle, roll it up.

Cut into slices, and leave to cool fully on a cooling rack before packing in the lunchbox.

Top Tip!

Don't leave your omelette wraps to cool completely before rolling up or they will be much harder to roll.

You'll have ticked off carbs, protein and possibly dairy with this recipe, so pack your omelette wraps alongside some fruit and veg and you're all set!

DIY Fajita Lunch

This idea is perfect when you have either leftover roast chicken or, even better, leftover fajita mix from the night before. In fact, next time you make fajitas, why not put a little of the filling in a tub in the fridge there and then, and you'll have a super easy lunch ready to go in the morning.

When I first packed this lunch for my son, I would pack it completely plain with just cold leftover roast chicken and raw red peppers. So if your child prefers their food dry and plain – start that way and introduce additional flavours as time goes on.

You'll need

OPTION 1
- 1 tortilla wrap
- Leftover fajita mix

OPTION 2
- 1 tortilla wrap
- Leftover roast chicken
- Red pepper
- OPTIONAL: mild peri-peri dipping sauce or peri-peri mayo

Top Tip!
Don't forget to include a small fork and/or spoon if the mixture is messy.

What to do

OPTION 1
Use a circular cookie cutter to cut your tortilla wrap into smaller circles. The size of cutter you'll need will depend on the size of the section where you're going to pack them in your lunchbox.

Add your leftover fajita filler to another section of your lunchbox.

OPTION 2
If you have no leftover fajita mix, in a small bowl, shred some leftover roast chicken and add a little mild peri-peri sauce – mix until evenly coated. Add to another section of your lunchbox.

Thinly slice some red peppers and add to a third section.

For both options, show your child how they can fill their own mini-wraps at lunchtime.

You'll have packed carbs, protein and possibly veggies and dairy too, so add some fruit and job's a good'un.

STARTING THE WEEK STRONG

Mega Sandwich Swirls

Lunchbox Formula Checklist
Grains/Carbs ✓
+
Protein ☐
+
Dairy ☐
+
Fruit ☐
+
Vegetable ☐

If you looked at the roll-ups on page 44 and thought 'PAH – they need more than THAT', then this is the hack for you! These are the same idea, but bigger, for bigger appetites.

You'll need

- 2 slices of bread
- Your chosen sandwich filler

What to do

Remove all crusts if needed or, if not, just the top crust of each slice.

Place the top edges together, overlapping by about a couple of centimetres.

Roll the bread all flat, while squashing the overlap to seal the two slices together as one extra long roll.

Add your filling.

Roll from one short end, all the way to the other.

Cut into 3 to 4 slices for extra large, chunky sandwich swirls for hungry eaters.

If you've got a hungry sandwich eater, chances are you've managed a good couple of food groups in the sandwich swirls. Add your remaining food groups to your lunchbox, and you are done.

A Note on Crusts

One of the questions I'm asked most online is: what do I do with the 'wasted' bread from removing crusts. And I always reply that it's only a waste IF you waste them.

If you have a child who will eat the crusts, then don't remove them— that is a waste! I rarely take crusts off anything I make for my son, as he WILL eat them. In fact, the ten-year-old version of him hoovers up the crusts on the chopping board in the morning while I'm making his sister's lunch — so that's one excellent way of preventing crust-waste right there!

But, on the other hand, my daughter genuinely does not like crusts. And yes, maybe I 'should' make her eat them. But, honestly, it's taken so long for her to even like sandwiches that I would far rather she ate the rest of the sandwich, with the goodness of all that bread and the filling inside, than worry over a few slithers of crust that I've cut off. But if you're cutting out sandwich shapes and are potentially 'wasting' much more than just the crusts, then it's worth considering using them up in one of these three ways.

1. Salad Croutons

Simply cut your crusts and offcuts into small chunks, mix in some melted butter and/or olive oil and add any flavouring you like — garlic granules and oregano are my favourite, or even a simple twist of salt and pepper. You can then either airfry for a few minutes, shaking regularly. Or, next time you have the oven on, pop them on a baking tray in a single layer and bake until golden brown but not dark or burned. Use your crunchy fresh croutons straight away, or seal in an airtight container for a couple of days at room temperature.

> **Top Tip!**
> If I know I'm planning to save the offcuts, I cut the shapes out of plain bread, then butter and fill them afterwards — otherwise you might end up with bits of all kinds of fillings left in your offcuts, which could get rather gross.

2. Jam Donut French Toast Bites

These are perfect if you've been making jam sandwiches and have jammy offcuts. Beat an egg and add a splosh of milk and a couple of drops of vanilla extract. Chop the jammy sandwich offcuts into chunks the size of a 50p piece, then add to a bowl and give them a good toss to ensure they're eggy all over.

Melt some butter in a large frying pan then tip the jammy, eggy bread into the pan and allow to cook, tossing regularly. When they're beginning to look cooked, with little brown patches, sprinkle in a teaspoon of sugar and stir again. Allow the sugar to melt and make them all a bit caramelised. Either serve immediately or, if you're feeling particularly decadent, serve and then sprinkle on a little more sugar for the crunch factor.

> **Top Tip!**
> These are delicious served with berries and thick creamy yoghurt.

3. Breadcrumbs

Blitz your leftover crusts in a food processor until fine, then either keep in an airtight container for a couple of days, or in the freezer until needed. Fresh breadcrumbs are brilliant to mix in with cheese and a little salt and pepper to sprinkle on top of pasta bakes for a lovely crunchy topping.

End of the Week
Getting through Thursday & Friday

However much we know it's coming, and however much we plan, or intend to plan for it, the end of the week creeps up on us and the fresh food runs out! If you're anything like me, there will be weeks (most in my case) where you'll find yourself, come Thursday and Friday, in the kitchen trying to pack lunches with no obvious lunchbox food around.

I hope that the following lunch ideas save you the stress of staring into an empty lunchbox and wanting to cry – I've done all the thinking for you, you just need a few freezer friends stashed away ready to call on in your moment of need.

Next time you have bread or bakery products that you know no one will finish, rather than leaving them to go off completely before chucking them out (come on, we've all done it!), toss them into the freezer now. Or better yet, for the organised among us – whenever you buy them, keep some out and put a few slices or portions in the freezer straight away; this way you know they're at their freshest when you need to call on them in the future.

Look out for (and freeze):

- Pitta breads
- Wraps
- Croissants (slice before freezing)
- Bagels (slice before freezing)
- Sliced bread (or slice before freezing as it defrosts a lot quicker than an unsliced loaf)

Pizza Quesadillas

If you haven't heard of a quesadilla before – think cheese toastie but made with a wrap instead of sliced bread, and you'll pretty much get the picture. You can add loads of fancy fillings, but like a toastie, it's the cheese that literally holds it all together. We like a mix of extra mature Cheddar for flavour and Double Gloucester for its butteriness. We're a pizza kinda household, so our quesadillas get pizzafied!

You'll need

- 1 tortilla wrap (or 2 mini ones) – fresh or frozen
- Cheese
- A little pizza sauce
- Your child's favourite pizza toppings: a great way to sneak veggies in, if they'll allow it!

What to do

Make sure you have a frying pan which is big enough for your tortilla wrap to lie flat. If you only have a smaller pan, use two mini wraps.

Add pizza sauce to one half of your tortilla wrap (colour in a semicircle with sauce). If you're using mini wraps, add sauce to one whole mini wrap.

Top the sauce with your cheese and pizza toppings (no raw meats – sandwich meats are fine, but bacon etc needs to be cooked first).

Fold the naked half over the filling, and press down gently.

Lunchbox Formula Checklist

Grains/Carbs ✓
+
Protein ✓
+
Dairy ✓
+
Fruit ☐
+
Vegetable ☐

Top Tip!

Freeze your favourite pizza sauce in an ice cube tray, then just defrost a tiny bit whenever needed. Or for a quick fix just mix a small teaspoon of tomato puree with a tiny squirt of ketchup and a pinch of oregano.

Pop your creation in the pan and put it on a medium heat – you want to melt the cheese without burning the wrap.

After a minute or two, check the bottom to see if it's lightly browned, then flip over and cook long enough to brown the other side.

Once toasted both sides, and melted through the middle, transfer to a cooling rack and cool fully before chopping and packing.

Your quesadilla will tick off your carbs, dairy and protein, so add some fruit and veg and perhaps a crunchy treat, and you're good to go!

Cheese Toastie Roll-Ups

Nobody enjoys a sandwich made with stale bread. And when you've got a child who isn't convinced about sandwiches anyway, giving them a dry sandwich (a) will probably mean they won't eat it and (b) might even make them decide they don't like sandwiches at all now . . . not ideal!

BUT turning it into a toastie roll-up makes even stale bread tasty again. And – bonus! – my fussy eaters have always accepted melted cheese (even that has cooled back down) much better than any other cheese in their lunch. You can always try these warm at home first to see whether they hit the spot.

You'll need

- 1 or 2 slices of bread
- Cheese
- A little butter/spread/olive oil
- OPTIONAL: any extra toastie fillings
- A rolling pin

What to do

Remove bread crusts (if needed).

Roll the bread flat with a rolling pin – this makes the toasties easier to roll up tightly.

Add grated cheese over the top and roll up tight. I go from bottom to top, rather than side to side as this makes the roll-ups a little bigger in the end.

Add some butter or oil to a frying pan on a medium heat and place the roll-ups in with the open edge downwards – this helps them to seal shut while cooking.

Once browned, and not unrolling, keep turning them over to cook on all sides.

Cool thoroughly on a wire cooling tray before packing, or enjoy them warm at home!

If they go down well a few times, with just cheese inside, try mixing it up with additional fillings too – a slice of ham or pepperoni or some finely chopped veggies.

You've packed carbs and dairy or protein, so just add your fruit and veggies and you're all set!

Top Tip!

If packing for younger children, sausages can be choking hazards, so split the sausage lengthways before popping in the roll.

Mini Hot Dogs

My kids go nuts for these, and I promise the little extra effort is not too taxing, especially when you've run out of bread anyway. To be honest, it's much quicker than an impromptu dash to the shop AND you can do it in your PJs while drinking tea. Which counts as a win for me!

You'll need

- 100g self-raising flour
- 115g plain fromage frais (or Greek yoghurt)
- Cocktail sausages or leftover (cooked) chipolatas

What to do

These can be cooked in the oven or airfryer. If using the oven, preheat to 180°C fan.

Weigh out your flour and fromage frais into a small mixing bowl, or a large cereal bowl.

Use a spoon to bring them together into a dough, then once it's pretty much mixed it's easier to simply stick your hands in and knead it together until smooth.

Roll into a sausage shape, then cut in half. Next, divide each half into roughly thirds. (If you're of a precise persuasion, they should each weigh around 30 to 35g.)

With some extra flour on your hands, use the board to roll the dough balls into round or slightly oval shapes – they should look something like mini hot dog buns.

Lunchbox Formula Checklist

- Grains/Carbs ✓
- \+ Protein ✓
- \+ Dairy ☐
- \+ Fruit ☐
- \+ Vegetable ☐

Top Tip!

Cocktail sausages can usually be frozen (double check your brand), so next time you see a big tub on offer, grab them, pop enough for a couple of days in the fridge and freeze the rest! Super handy to have on hand, and can be packed from frozen and will defrost by lunchtime.

AIRFRYER: Pop them in the airfryer (a reusable liner helps them not to stick if you have one), and turn it to 200°C (no need to preheat) for 10 minutes. Unstick the rolls from the liner, then flip over and cook them on the other side for 2 minutes more.

OVEN: Place on a non-stick baking tray or tray liner, and bake for 15 minutes.

Once cooked they need to cool FULLY before you add the sausages. Place on a cooling rack, so they don't get sweaty bottoms!

Slice a deep slit down the middle of the top – like a hot dog roll – and pop a cocktail sausage inside.

You'll have ticked carbs and protein off your checklist, so you just need to grab your other food groups now.

Pancake Lunchables

We make these pancakes hot for breakfast some school mornings when I'm feeling particularly delusional about how much time we'll need to get everyone out of the house on time. If you make palm-sized ones for breakfast you can then use any leftover batter to make smaller, 3 to 4 cm ones, and cool them to serve that day. Or if you run out of time, save the batter in the fridge and fry them up later. Leftover cooked pancakes can be frozen and packed straight from the freezer. Mega win!

You'll need

- 150g self-raising flour
- 1 tsp baking powder
- 150ml milk
- 1 egg (large is best, but medium is fine if that's what you've got in)

What to do

Whisk the flour and baking powder together in a small mixing bowl.

Measure out your milk into a jug then add the egg. Whisk these together.

Pour the wet mix into the dry and whisk together until smooth and your batter has no visible lumps.

Heat a non-stick frying pan over a medium/high heat and let the pan get hot for a minute or so.

Add a little butter, spread or oil and spread it around the surface, then pour small circles of batter into the pan.

Fry for a minute or so and when the edges begin to look cooked, peek underneath to check they're lightly browned underneath.

Flip them all over and cook the other sides for another minute before tipping onto a cooling rack to cool before packing.

These pancakes count just as the carbs section of your checklist, but you can think of them as little vehicles for other toppings – like a cracker – and pack with some sliced cheese, or small pieces of sandwich meat. My daughter especially likes them packed alongside some fried, cooled chorizo. And yet she won't eat a ham sandwich . . . go figure.

Nacho Average Thursday

Go freezer diving for any flat, savoury bakery products and let's turn them from bland to buttery, garlicky and crispy! We use pitta bread, mini naan bread and crumpets mainly for our nachos, but there's not a lot I can't imagine them working with.

You'll need

- 1 pitta bread, mini naan bread or crumpet – fresh or defrosted if frozen
- EITHER: 5 to 10g butter and a pinch of garlic granules
- OR: 5 to 10g store-bought garlic butter
- 1 tsp olive oil

What to do

Melt your butter or garlic butter in the microwave then add the oil with a decent pinch of garlic granules (if not using garlic butter) and a little salt and pepper. Then mix well.

Cut your pitta or naan bread into strips about 4 to 5 cm wide, and then cut these down into lots of little triangles. If using crumpets, cut them into 8 portions like a pizza.

Add your tiny triangles to the butter bowl and use a pastry brush to mix and coat them all with the garlicky buttery goodness. Make sure all sides get a good covering.

Pop them in the airfryer at 180 to 200°C for 3 to 5 minutes, shaking the basket regularly. Stop when they look lightly toasted and golden brown – but before they're brown all over.

Tip out onto a cooling rack and allow to cool fully while packing the rest of your lunchbox.

You can, of course, make these in the oven. Just add them to a baking tray (non-stick if you have one) and bake them in the oven at 180°C for 7 to 10 minutes until nicely toasted.

Lunchbox Formula Checklist

- Grains/Carbs ✓
- \+ Protein ☐
- \+ Dairy ☐
- \+ Fruit ☐
- \+ Vegetable ☐

Top Tip!

If you're sending these for the first time and have a fussy eater (or two), then I'd recommend trying them out first at home, so they know what to expect at school. If they try them and aren't convinced, send a few alongside some crackers or oatcakes, so they have the opportunity to try again, but you also know they won't go hungry if they're still not sure.

Your nachos tick off your carbs for today, so pair them with a snacky protein source, like chunks of chicken, a hard-boiled egg or some cheese, along with the other food groups from your checklist.

Porridge Flapjacks

My daughter has eaten these since the long-ago days of weaning, but she still enjoys them hot and cold, and they're still a total cheap, easy, healthy win! I've included some optional extras to make them a bit more exciting and varied if you have an older child who enjoys a little more flavour and texture these days.

You'll need

- 35g oats
- 50ml milk (we use whole milk)
- OPTIONAL, but extra nutritious if you have it: a pinch of ground flaxseed

Tasty extras

- Cocoa powder and honey (not for children under one)
- Seed butter (or nut butter if eating at home), alone or with jam
- Mashed banana
- Berries – blueberries are always brilliant in flapjacks

Lunchbox Formula Checklist

Grains/Carbs ✓
+
Protein ☐
+
Dairy ✓
+
Fruit ☐
+
Vegetable ☐

What to do

Tip the oats and flaxseed onto a small plate (or a flat cereal bowl or plastic tub if needed, but nothing metal) and mix with a teaspoon.

Add milk and mix until all the oats are coated in the milk.

Add any tasty extras, mix well and lightly squash down so you get an even surface.

Pop in the microwave for 2 minutes on full power, then remove and leave to cool.

Once the mixture has cooled for a couple of minutes, slide a knife or spoon under your flapjack to shimmy it off the plate. Fold it in half (sticky sides together) and cut in half or into slices, and leave to fully cool before packing.

Top Tip!

Feel free to experiment with your tasty extras! You can't go too far wrong with flapjacks . . .

Kiddie Charcuterie

Is there anything better than those days between Christmas and New Year, when you fill your plate with crackers, cheese, chutney, fruit, crisps and basically anything else that's left over from Christmas? Well, you can totally use that Twixmas platter as inspiration for a kid's packed lunch too.

This kind of lunch is best with a bento box that seals each section, or you need to aim for drier foods that won't leak onto other bits and make them sad and soggy.

Here's how we like to do it . . .

You'll need

- Crackers
- Cheese (any they like either in little cubes, or sliced for crackers, or perhaps a couple of star shapes to make it look extra fun and fancy)
- Ham/leftover roast chicken/pepperoni, etc
- Fruits (grapes, peeled satsumas, berries, dried apricots, etc)
- Veggies (carrot sticks, cucumber, sliced peppers, etc)
- Any dips they like – such as hummus
- Olives (make sure they're destoned, and cut in half if needed)
- Snacky treats like pretzels and veggie sticks

What to do

Use your lunchbox formula checklist to make sure you're packing snacky bits from all the food groups, and this one should be packed up in a few minutes flat. Get the kettle on, you deserve it!

Top Tip!

Why not try cutting your scones into other fun shapes too – we make mini star ones which look really cute in a lunchbox. Alternatively, don't faff about with cutters at all. Instead, simply chop the dough into squares or triangles with a knife and get on with your life!

Easy Peasy Cheesy Scones

Lunchbox Formula Checklist
- Grains/Carbs ✓
- \+ Protein ☐
- \+ Dairy ✓
- \+ Fruit ☐
- \+ Vegetable ☐

Tell me anything that's better than a fresh, buttered cheese scone . . . I'll wait!

Scones are best on the day you make them. BUT if you freeze them that same day, they won't have time to get stale overnight. Cut them in half before freezing, so you can butter them as soon as they come out the freezer.

For 'proper' scones, I use butter, but on school mornings I use soft baking spread because it speeds up the process. Plus, if you have a stand mixer, you can use that with the paddle attachment, rather than faffing about rubbing the butter and flour together with your fingers while someone hangs off your leg and declares that they NEED Frosties.

You'll need

- 225g self-raising flour
- 30g baking spread (or upgrade to butter if you're not in a hurry)
- Pinch of nutmeg
- Pinch of mustard powder
- Salt and pepper
- 150g cheese (my favourite for the kids is a good strong Cheddar inside the scones and then more Cheddar or double Gloucester on top)
- 120ml milk

What to do

Get your oven heating to 220°C fan, and line a baking tray with a non-stick baking mat.

Put your baking spread (or butter) in a mixing bowl with your flour, nutmeg, mustard powder and a little salt and pepper. Rub them together with your fingertips, or stand mixer, until there's no lumps of spread and the texture resembles breadcrumbs.

Add ¾ of your cheese (or just your stronger one, if using two kinds) and mix with a knife until evenly distributed.

Pour in most of your milk and mix with the knife until it comes together as a dough – if it's still a bit crumbly add the last of the milk.

Tip your mixture out onto a pre-floured board and gently squash flat-ish with the heels of your hand until it's about 3 to 4 cm thick. Or use a rolling pin if there's one to hand. Use a 5 cm cookie cutter to cut into circles and place them on the baking tray, leaving enough space for them to grow a little in the oven.

Cut out as many as you can, then gently bring the dough back to a ball and squash flat again before cutting some more. Repeat as needed.

Bake in the oven for around 10 minutes. They'll cook quicker the smaller they are, so trust your nose timer and if you can smell them – check on them!

Garlic Toast Bites

These are basically croutons, but in fussy-eater speak! My kids would have been immediately suspicious of croutons, but toast bites? Now you're talking! I know croutons doesn't sound like a 'main' for a meal, but go with me.

These came about from having a fussy eater who doesn't love a sandwich on the best of days, let alone when the bread is tending towards questionable by the end of the week. BUT she does love garlic bread, and anything crispy. Add melted garlic butter to cubes of stale bread, and bish, bash, bosh you've saved bread from the bin and made lunch for just a few pence. Pair it with the rest of the food groups, and it's the same as a fancy sandwich by the time it makes it into their bellies.

You'll need

- Any bread – fresh if you have it, a bit stale if that's all you've got
- 15g butter/spreadable butter
- ½ tsp garlic granules or a little chopped or pre-chopped garlic
- Salt and pepper
- OPTIONAL: a teaspoon of olive oil helps make them extra crispy!
- CHEAT: use store-bought garlic butter

What to do

Remove the crusts if needed, then cut your bread into little squares or chunks (or shapes if you're feeling extra fancy).

Lunchbox Formula Checklist
- Grains/Carbs ✓
- Protein ☐
- Dairy ☐
- Fruit ☐
- Vegetable ☐

Melt your butter in a small cereal bowl (one big enough to hold all your bread in the next step) in the microwave.

Add the garlic – granules or chopped – plus salt, pepper and oil (if using), and mix.

Add the bread chunks and mix together to coat all the bread.

Pop in the airfryer at 200°C (no need to preheat) for 3 to 5 minutes, stopping to shake the basket regularly and stopping once they look golden brown but not burned.

Cool fully on a cooling rack before packing (or they'll be soggy by lunch).

You absolutely can cook these in the oven too, it's just less economical to heat a whole oven for a slice of bread, but you can always do it if the oven is on anyway, then cool fully and stash for the next day. Preheat your oven to 180°C fan and bake until lightly toasted for 7 to 10 minutes, flipping halfway through.

Only carbs ticked off for this one, so fill the rest of their lunchbox accordingly to balance it out.

Cheat Sausage Rolls

> **Lunchbox Formula Checklist**
> Grains/Carbs ✓
> +
> Protein ✓
> +
> Dairy ☐
> +
> Fruit ☐
> +
> Vegetable ☐

This one will only save you if you either have some ready-rolled pastry in the fridge, or stashed in the freezer and defrost it the night before. If you haven't got either of those things – add it to next week's shopping list now and know it will be ready and waiting to save you next week instead!

These cheat sausage rolls can be frozen before baking IF you haven't already frozen the pastry at any point, or after baking if you have.

You'll need

- A sheet of ready-rolled puff pastry
- Cocktail sausages (fresh or defrosted)
- A splash of milk

Top Tip!
You can of course use mini veggie sausages to make these.

What to do

Preheat your airfryer to 200°C (or put your fan oven on at the same temperature).

Roll out your pastry keeping it on the backing paper, then use a pizza cutter to cut a few thin (less than one centimetre) strips.

Take a cocktail sausage and tightly wind the pastry strip around the sausage from one end to the other.

Repeat for however many you'd like to make. I tend to pack 3 to 4 per child.

Brush with a little milk, then bake in the airfryer for 10 to 12 minutes until golden brown and the pastry is no longer soggy. If you cook these in the oven, they will take a little longer.

Transfer to a cooling rack and allow to cool fully before packing for lunch.

These cheat sausage rolls tick off carbs and protein, so just add some dairy and any fruit or veg and you're good to go. Remember the cheat sheets on pages 19 and 20 if you're stumped for ideas.

Winter

Winter Solstice (21/22 Dec)
Christmas
Hanukkah
New Year's Eve & Day
Popcorn Day (19 Jan)
Burns Night (25 Jan)
Chinese New Year
Valentine's Day (14 Feb)

Spring

St Patrick's Day (17 Mar)
Spring Equinox (21 Mar)
April Fool's Day (1 Apr)
National Unicorn Day (9 Apr)
Star Wars Day (4 May)

Summer

Pride Week (June)
Father's Day (3rd Sunday in June)
Summer Solstice (20/21 June)
Harry Potter's birthday (31 July)
School holidays

Autumn

Back to school
Roald Dahl Day (13 Sep)
Autumn Equinox (23 Sep)
World Smile Day (4 Oct)
Halloween (31 Oct)
Guy Fawkes Night (5 Nov)
Remembrance Day (11 Nov)

Dates that move

Children In Need Day
Mother's Day (4th Sunday of Lent)
Easter
Eid al-Fitr
Diwali
Pancake Day
Red Nose Day

Add your own dates

Themed Lunches

For when you feel a bit extra

If you're anything like me, you'll feel like you need a creative outlet once in a while. And while there isn't always time for solo hobbies in early motherhood, I promise that there is joy to be found in the depths of a lunchbox. You can use these themed lunches to surprise your little one at school — I love imagining their excited faces when opening the box! — but it's also lovely to get them involved in the creative side too . . . you might be surprised by the ideas they have!

Themed lunches are perfect when something special is in the calendar for everyone: Valentine's, Easter, Christmas and so on; or when it's a special date just for your child: their birthday or a special achievement. And, of course, they're also fabulous for absolutely no reason at all — just because!

If you need a cheat sheet, these calendar dates are a nice, easy starting point. Feel free to add to this with birthdays or other celebrations your family enjoys.

Valentine's Day

Nothing is cuter than a 'love-day' themed lunch! Just think of anything red or pink that your child will happily eat and anything you can cut into heart shapes. Or, of course, you can buy snacks that already have hearts on them – like a certain jammy biscuit, for example.

This is one themed lunch you might want to crack out early in the primary school years when your child still thinks this the loveliest thing you could do for them, because trust me, the time will come when you suggest Mummy making a lovely love-heart sandwich for them and you will be met with 'THE LOOK'. You know the one: the face that says loud and clear, 'Could you be any more embarrassing?', often accompanied with an eye roll and a sigh of exasperation. Isn't parenthood just the gift that keeps on giving?

Anyway, for those young innocent souls who will enjoy opening a box of love, here are some ideas!

Top Tip!

If Valentine's falls in the half-term holiday – just pop everything on a board or a big plate and let everyone dig in together. You never know, you might even get away with this non-school-based love-lunch for longer! I've found that the key to making a sharing platter look its best is to fill as much blank space as possible – simply put, use a smaller board and cram it all in!

Some ideas to include:

- Heart strawberries – see page 28
- Heart sausages – see page 31
- Heart sandwiches – made using a heart-shaped cutter
- Pretzels (including chocolate-covered ones if you're at home or chocolate is allowed at school)
- Heart-themed sweets and biscuits
- Use a tiny heart-shaped veg cutter to add some heart-themed goodness!

Or, if you want a show stopper main, try this Love Letter Sandwich . . .

Disclaimer: This is an idea that I saw online – and I absolutely had to have a go at making it!

You'll need

- 2 slices of bread
- Your filling of choice, but something sticky works best (cheese spread, or jam perhaps)
- A raspberry

What to do

Remove the crusts from both slices of bread.

Using a medium-sized sharp knife, cut the top third off one slice of bread (on the bigger piece).

Make two more cuts from the top corners into the centre so your bread is now shaped, like the opening of an envelope (shown in the illustrations on the next page).

On the other slice of bread, add your filling to the bottom half making sure to leave an empty border around the edge and bottom.

Place the smaller piece (the opening of the envelope we just cut) on top of the filling, lining up the bottom and side edges.

Next, we're going to cut the top flap of the envelope. Line your knife up at the top points of the top piece of bread, facing diagonally up, into the centre of the bottom slice of bread, like this:

Do the same on the other side.

Now we need to seal the edges. Turn your knife over, and use the non-sharp edge of the blade to press a line down each edge and the base of the sandwich.

Top Tip!

If you find using the back of the knife isn't successful, then try a bamboo skewer and press down along that. This creates a slightly wider sealed area, which can be stronger. If often depends on the type of bread you're using.

Use the sharp blade to score two lines from the bottom corners into the centre of your V-shaped dip, creating an authentic envelope look.

Then score another a line where the envelope should fold. Fold the flap down and give it a little squash and it should hold in place. If it doesn't, you might need to add a little extra of your sticky filling a little higher up.

Cut your raspberry in half and cut a small V shape out of the top of one half, and place it on the sealed point of the envelope like a wax stamp. If you're sending this for lunch at school, then add a little jam or chocolate spread to stick the raspberry in place.

FRONT SLICE

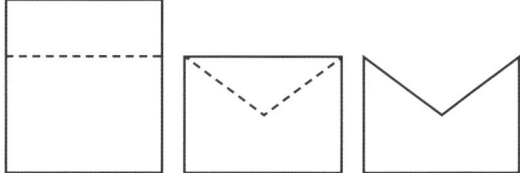

BACK SLICE

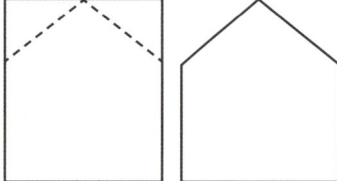

Happy Birthday

How excited do primary school kids get about having their birthday AT school? Is that a thing with your kid(s) too? As a bit of fun, I once asked my son which he would prefer: to go to the zoo with me, on his sixth birthday, or to spend it at school? He actually choose school. He said he wanted to be there and hand out his sweets. I know! I wasn't offended at all . . .

Easiest idea

Use the age they're turning as the theme for their lunchbox that day.

You can create birthday sandwiches with their new age punched out the top, and a fun filling like jam that shows the cut-out number up well!

Continue the theme with the age as the number of everything else in the lunchbox. For example, they're turning 5, so 5 mini biscuits, 5 mini breadsticks, 5 cucumber crowns, 5 strawberry hearts . . . you get the idea! As they get older you can simply chop things smaller so they still, for example, get 9 of everything without you having to pack way too much food.

And, if you really want to run with this theme, then 7 is a super fun age because you can easily make foods into a 7 shape.

Here's a number 7 chocolate finger biscuit for you to try . . .

Take two chocolate finger biscuits and cut a 45-degree diagonal line just above halfway on each, but in opposite directions, like this:

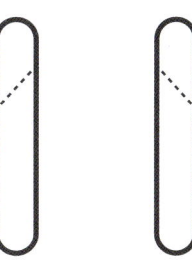

THEMED LUNCHES

Take the bottom of the first biscuit, and the top of the second and place the cut edges together. And ta-dah! You have formed a number 7 shape.

To stick them together you'll need some edible glue or a tiny bit of melted chocolate. If you don't have edible glue, take one piece of milk chocolate and heat a small frying pan for 30 seconds on the hob. Turn the heat off and hold the square of chocolate touching the pan for a few seconds until the edge melts. Take this and wipe the melted chocolate onto one cut biscuit end, then press the two cut sides together and leave to dry. Feel free to enjoy any leftovers yourself. (Chef's perk!)

This 7 cut works with any long thin food, so try it on cocktail sausages or mini pepperoni sausages – these are best held together with a cocktail stick.

Taking birthday lunches a step further

If you've done this a couple of times and want to get extra fancy, try using a fondant stamp* and some edible ink pens to make the prettiest sandwiches the birthday boy or girl has ever had!

You'll need

- 1 or 2 slices of white or 50/50 bread
- Your choice of sandwich filling (I recommend sending their absolute favourite on their birthday, if school allows)
- Fondant stamp
- Edible ink pens or cake pens
- A circle cutter, if you have one; if not, this idea works on square sandwiches too

What to do

Cut your bread into the desired shape – small enough to fit where you need it to fit in the lunchbox, but big enough for the stamp.

Colour the stamp, then flip it over and press firmly onto the top slice of bread. Press down all over the area with the coloured-in design, then carefully peel off the bread to reveal your creation.

Make the rest of your sandwich as normal, then pop your colourful bread on the top before packing.

Feel free to get as creative as you want with your stamp colouring. Use a mix of other colours from your themed lunch (perhaps a whole lunch of their favourite colour for their birthday), a different colour for each word on the stamp, or colour a pattern across the words, like the rainbow design pictured.

* I get mine from etsy; just search 'fondant stamp birthday' and you'll find lots of options.

Top Tip!

Use your edible ink pens to colour the stamp BEFORE using it on the bread. This ensures the colour stamps really neatly, in all the right places, and is so much easier and more effective than doing it the other way round.

Easter Eggstravaganza

Obviously, Easter Sunday never falls on a school day, but I like making these ideas in the run-up to the Easter holidays as it adds to the excitement as we build up to the holidays.

An egg-shaped cutter can be tricky to come by, but if you keep an eye out in the bargain shops during the Easter period you should be able to pick one up. And, of course, bunnies are the other option for cutters.

Easter Lunch - Boiled Egg Chickie

So much Easter food aimed at children is the unhealthy stuff, so here's a super cute, healthy Easter egg, perfect for school lunches. When I first put one of these chickies in my son's lunchbox, he came home and told me that his friend said his mum turns 'food into toys'. What a great compliment; I loved it. Admittedly, these are a little fiddly, but they are worth the effort — I guarantee the kids will think they're adorable!

You'll need

- Eggs
- A sharp knife with a small blade (see recommendation on page 12)
- Cake pens or edible ink pens

What to do

Place your eggs in a pan of boiling water for 9 minutes. Cool the eggs in some super cold tap water (add ice if you have it, but don't worry if not, just replace the cold water a couple of times, once it heats up) to stop the eggs cooking any further. This is important — it will help make sure your yolks stay yellow like a chick (and don't turn that funny greenish-grey colour).

Once cool enough to handle, peel and remove all of the shell.

Use the point of your sharp knife to cut a line of tiny zigzags about halfway up the egg. Push the knife in gently and you should be able to feel the yolk — cut down as deep as the yolk, while trying not to cut into it too much.

Cut another zigzag line about 1 cm or so underneath the first, then cut a small curved line to join top to bottom.

Use the tip of the sharp knife to peel away the zigzag window. If it doesn't come away cleanly, pause and check all of your zigzag lines have cut deeply enough through the egg white.

> **Top Tip!**
> When you first insert the knife, if you can feel the hard yolk right under the surface, stop and turn the egg round, and try on that side.

Using your cake pens, add little black eyes and an orange triangle for the beak. Then it's time to say hi to your new chickie friend!

Haunted Halloween

Halloween oftens falls in the October half-term holiday, which means no school rules for lunches and picnics. So, the ideas below reflect that! If you want to send a Halloween lunch on a school day – then just use the ideas that are school friendly.

My biggest tip for Halloween food is to buy a pack of edible eyes, which you can find in the homebaking section at the supermarket. Add them to everything and you'll have instant spookiness. Reusable eye food picks are great here too, as are my trusty edible ink pens for drawing ghoulish faces. If you want to make savoury edible eyes, then you can use a drinking straw to cut tiny circles of boiled egg white and add a dot of edible ink pen, or a small black seed, to make the pupils!

For a spooktastic Halloween picnic

Make ghost sandwiches from half a slice of bread (or two ghosts from a full sandwich).

Make your sandwich and remove the crusts. If you're making two ghosts, cut your sandwich in half as normal.

Then using a small glass, press a curved edge on one end of the sandwich. Use a sharp knife to cut along the curved line, then cut a zigzag line at the other end to make your ghostie sandwich(es).

Add edible eyes to bring your ghost to life, and if you want to cut a peek-a-boo mouth, use the drinking straw of a kids' bottle to cut through the top layer of bread before assembling your sandwich ghost.

Add edible eyes to everything else you pack to keep it on theme. Round snacks make great spooky faces – extra points if you can add a mouth with fangs too.

Halloween Platter

If you're hosting a Halloween party, look out for a large black dinner plate as your central serving board – this adds instant drama and spookiness and will make your colourful food POP!

Buy foods in as many colours as possible. Look out for Halloween specials with spooky shapes or packaging and add eyes to everything else.

- Turn peeled clementines into pumpkins with a little baton of cucumber or celery in the top as a stalk.
- Add mini marshmallows to raspberries to look like toadstools for witches' potions.
- Draw ghostly faces on marshmallows with edible ink pens.
- Look out for crisps that come in fun shapes – faces, aliens, claws . . . Lot of supermarkets do themed pretzels for Halloween too.
- If you've bought a set of vegetable cutters, you may have a little mushroom-shaped one, which can be easily turned into tiny skulls by adding some little eye holes.

Remember the kids will probably be getting plenty of sugar throughout Halloween, so focus on fruits, vegetables, protein and low sugar carbohydrate food to fill them with some goodness before they get started on the sweets.

Lunchboxes that last!

A friend of mine recently mentioned how pleased she is that her 16-year-old has always had a packed lunch from home, because it's just normal for her, so while her friends might pop to the shop and make impulsive food choices, she is still content with a balanced meal from home.

First Day of School

I was going to offer you first day of school and back to school lunches as one and the same, but then I realised that they are absolutely not the same! Your child's first day of school is such an important moment. Whether it's your first baby going off into the big wide world, or you're a seasoned pro-parent who knows the drill, it's the end of an era for the both of you – and the start of their new life as a school kid.

A note on school dinners for new school starters

Some kids will bounce into school not looking back and will skip down to lunch to tuck into their first ever school hot dinner without hesitation, and that's great (especially as those hot dinners are free). BUT if you know that school lunches will cause your child additional worry, then please don't feel pressured into signing them up for school lunches because you feel like everyone else will, or because you 'should'. You know your child best, and if they need a box of familiar foods from home for a week, a month or even all year (and every year of their school lives to follow), then just do that! There is no right or wrong way, other than what is right or wrong for you and your child.

For us, that way is packed lunches. And yes, it took a while for my children to try school dinners, but I honestly don't mind. Lunch is one of the few things you and your child can control in their school day, so we embraced it and made it something special – think of it as a chance to send your chidren to school with an edible love note from home. Be cute, be fun, be as healthy and nourishing as you can, and just imagine their little faces when they open the box each day to see what you sent this time. (In the early years of school I would pack their lunch then show them it at home, explaining any sandwich fillings or different flavours, so they weren't worried come lunchtime.)

Equally, if you have a child who won't be fazed by the new dining experience, feel free to ignore this page and head through to explore some other ideas they might like more.

A note on mini cutters

As we've discovered, mini cutters are an easy, inexpensive way to make lunches super cute. They mean you can create something a little less overwhelming than a full hunk of sandwich and enable your child to eat a bit of this, and bit of that, which is perfect if they're feeling slightly nervous and unsure. I tend to keep everything little and nibbly for this reason; then they simply eat what they can manage.

> ### Back to School
>
> If your kids are anything like mine, back-to-school time is a mixture of excitement to get back to their friends, while knowing that once they're back, it's endless days of school routine for months on end. And that's why I don't tend to go all out on school-themed lunches. After all, I don't think kids need to open their lunchboxes and be reminded that life now is all about school: they know that — they're there! So instead, I tend to stick to their favourite foods, as a reassuring taste from home, then grab my letter and number cutters to cut out their new school year in their sandwich.

Christmas Cracker

The mental load at Christmas is eye-watering, so please don't look at this idea and think you're failing on any level if you're not making Christmas-themed packed lunches throughout December. BUT if your child is sticking with their packed lunch on Christmas dinner day at school, it can be fun to make it extra special. Here are a few suggestions of our favourite Christmas ideas – try one or two or go all out with a full festive lunchbox!

Rudolph Sandwiches

You'll need

- 2 to 4 slices of bread and your choice of sandwich filling
- 4 pretzels
- 4 edible eyes
- 2 Smarties or M&Ms
- Edible glue, icing or a tiny bit of nut-free chocolate spread

What to do

Make your sandwiches, then use a circular cookie cutter (or an upturned glass) to cut out two reindeer heads. Tuck the pretzels just inside the sandwich near the top to make antlers, then add the eyes and nose, sticking them on with your choice of 'glue'.

Top Tip!

If you're not allowed to send Smarties to school, even on a special occasion, try filling the sandwich with red jam and cutting out a hole for Rudolph's nose with a wide drinking straw to reveal the red jam underneath.

Festive Cucumber

Stack some slices of cucumber in a small section of your lunchbox, then cut holly leaves from two further slices and pop them on the top. Finish the effect with a red holly berry. A raspberry or the end of a strawberry is perfect for this.

If you haven't got a holly leaf cutter you can use a circle cutter and a drinking straw to cut your own. Use a circular cutter that's around the same diameter as your cucumber slice, then cut away a slither off each side of the cucumber to leave you with a pointed oval shape in the centre.

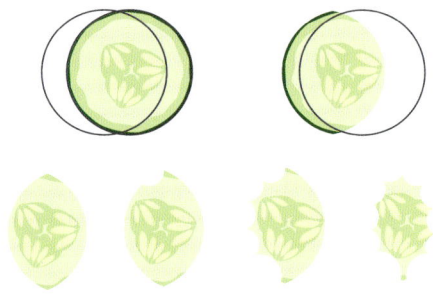

Then use a drinking straw to take a nibble out of the edges all the way around, in a holly leaf shape. Any bits of cucumber that get stuck in the straw can be shot out by blowing hard on the end – away from any food you intend to serve to others, obviously.

Strawberry Santa Hats

If school rules will allow a couple of mini marshmallows for a special festive lunch, top a couple of strawberries with a white mini marshmallow for all the Santa hat vibes! You can hold them in place with a cocktail stick, as long as your child is old enough to be sensible with one, or if not pack both separately and show your child how they can put them together at school and show all their friends!

Candy Cane Hot Dogs

This idea is for when you've got a bit of extra time on your hands one morning, or you're being very organised and prepping the night before.

Top Tip!

If you're making these for the under-sixes, slice your frankfurter lengthways before you begin and make it from just one half of a hot dog, to avoid it being a choking hazard.

You'll need

- 2 frankfurters
- Shop-bought, ready-rolled puff pastry or pizza dough
- Wooden cocktail sticks

What to do

Make a diagonal cut in the hot dog about a third of the length from the top. Then turn your knife the opposite way and cut a slightly less steep angle, about halfway up.

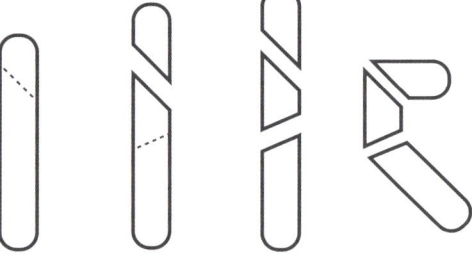

Turn the top piece over so it's touching the top of the middle piece with a bend and secure horizontally with a wooden cocktail stick. (Leave enough sticking out so that you can remove it after cooking.) Then turn the bottom piece over and do the same.

Cut your pastry or pizza dough into thin 5 mm slices using a pizza cutter, and wrap these slices around the frankfurter. You're aiming to create a candy cane effect, so leave a gap of sausage on show between the pastry or dough.

Bake in the oven at 180°C fan for 15 to 20 minutes until the dough is cooked through, or pop in the airfryer at 180°C for 10 to 15 minutes. Don't forget! Remove the cocktail stick! Serve hot at home or cool fully before packing for lunch.

Pirates Ahoy!

Ahoy there, matey! If yer in need of a fun lunch for yer kid, then follow these 'ere plans and the treasure shall be yers!

You'll need

- Sandwich thin with your choice of filling
- Edible ink pens
- Pretzels and mini pretzel sticks (or snap a big stick into little bits)
- A small carrot
- Some brightly coloured fruit
- A small round cheese (bonus marks if it comes in wax), or a snack stick of Cheddar, or a thick slice cut from a big block of Cheddar
- OPTIONAL: eye food picks, red ribbon or foil

1. TREASURE MAP
Fill your sandwich thin however you like, then, instead of cutting it, use your edible ink pens to draw a treasure map on top. Pop a little compass drawing in the corner for navigational effect, and don't forget the X to mark the spot!

2. PIRATE FRIEND
Round cheese option: Peel most of the wax from your round cheese, then use the edible ink pen to draw a pirate face on it, including an eyepatch!

Rectangular cheese option: Use your edible ink pens to draw your pirate face as above, or use a set of eye food picks for the face. Than add a red ribbon (or leftover chocolate foil) around the pirate's head as a bandana!

3. SKULL AND CROSSBONES
Arrange your pretzels and pretzel sticks like a skull and crossbones.

4. PIRATE TREASURE
Peel your carrot and cut it into thin circles to be your golden galleons.

Add some brightly coloured fruits as precious jewels and gems.

And yer treasure and map to find it now be completed, matey!

Over the Rainbow

Rainbows are so special to me. They were my son's 'favourite colour' from the moment he could talk, and for a long time everything in our house was rainbows. They are so bright and colourful that they instantly make you feel that little bit happier. So, let's look at some ideas for packing the most cheerful of colourful lunches!

You'll need

- 2 slices of bread
- Your choice of sandwich filling
- Edible ink pens
- A fruit or vegetable for every (or most) colours of the rainbow. I'd aim for red, orange, yellow, green, blue and purple
- A white(ish) coloured snack: for example, popcorn (if you don't need to worry about choking hazards), broken up rice cakes, or even mini marshmallows if you're packing a fun picnic rather than a school lunch (again, be aware of choking hazards)
- If you have lots of lunchbox options at your disposal – then go for a blue to feel like the sky!

What to do

Cut a large circle from each slice of bread with a 10 cm cookie cutter (or a wide glass).

Use a sharp knife to cut across the centre of each circle to make each into two semicircles. Keeping the circle halves together as a whole, use a small (2 to 3 cm) cutter to remove the very centre of the circle. (An upturned mini vegetable cutter is perfect for this, but if you don't have one, try a clean plastic bottle or wine bottle top.)

Use your edible ink pens to carefully colour a rainbow on one sandwich.

> **Top Tip!**
> Gently sweep the pen along the bread in a delicate brushing techinique, rather than as if you were colouring with a felt-tip pen.

Assemble your sandwiches with the rainbow bread on the very top.

Cut your fruits and vegetables into small batons, then layer them from red through to purple, across a couple of sections of your lunchbox.

Lastly add your 'white' snack as a little fluffy cloud in the sky.

RAINBOW CHEAT SHEET: Red, Orange, Yellow, Green, Blue, Indigo, Violet.

Ready, Steady, Go!

If you've got a child who loves to spend hours driving their toy cars and trucks around the place, then give this super easy vehicle-themed lunch a try!

You'll need

- A brioche roll works best but a small finger roll also works, if that's what they prefer
- Your choice of filling for the roll
- 1 slice of bread
- Fruit and veg in the colours of a traffic light
- 2 types of cheese: one orange, one light yellow (e.g. Red Leicester and mild Cheddar)
- Some 'hoop' cereal (chocolate if allowed at school)

What to do

1. CAR
Start by making your car sandwich. Slice your brioche roll in half (like you'd cut a burger bun, not along the top like a hot dog roll) and add your filling.

Cut 4 small circles from your slice of bread using a 4 cm cutter. If you have my recommended veggie cutter set, the biggest cutter used upside down, so it's circular not wiggly, is perfect, or you can use a small shot glass. Add a little butter to one side of the bread, then use this to stick them to the brioche bun as wheels.

2. TRAFFIC LIGHTS
Pack your red, orange and green fruits or veggies in stripes in one small section of your lunchbox to create a traffic light effect. Or go a step further by cutting them into small circles and stacking them in little columns of red at the top, orange in the middle and green at the bottom.

> **Top Tip!**
> Stacking the columns to the height of your lunchbox makes them less likely to move around on the way to school, as the box lid should help hold them in place.

3. TRAFFIC CONE
Cut a thick slice of each cheese and then stack both and cut into a long triangle shape, like a 2D traffic cone. Again, if you can make it the height of the section of your lunchbox it will fit snuggly and still look like a cone by lunchtime. Make two extra cuts across the triangle and then use the top and bottom of the orange cheese, and the middle of the yellow cheese, and stack them together to make your traffic cone shape.

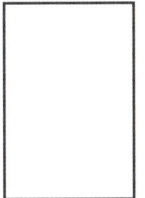 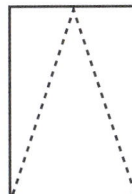 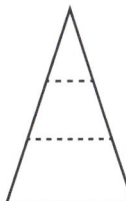

4. SPARE TYRES
Pop some chocolate hoops (or regular hoops) into the tiny middle section as some spare tyres and you're done!

Unicorn Magic

Nothing is more magical than unicorns, except perhaps when your child is young enough to really believe in unicorns – meaning you get to enjoy that unicorn magic with them through their eyes. Just now, I'm very sad that we seem to be coming out of this phase, even with my youngest. While I'm excited for whichever phase is coming next, please do make this unicorn lunch, not forgetting to tag me in it on Instagram . . . that way I can remember those good old magical unicorn days!

Top Tip!

Before you start cutting, double check your cutter fits your lunchbox. Trust the voice of experience here . . . if the cutter doesn't fit, your beautiful sandwich will get all squidged and lose a little of its sparkle!

You'll need

- 2 slices of light coloured bread
- Your choice of sandwich filling
- A unicorn cookie cutter
- A rainbow of fruits, vegetables and other snacks. If you missed that lesson in science, this is your cheat sheet: red, orange, yellow, green, blue, indigo, violet (let's just say purple)
- Cheese

What to do

Make your sandwich with both slices of bread, then use your unicorn cutter to carefully cut out your unicorn shape. Remember to push it through firmly then flip it over to make sure all the sharp edges have cut through the bread so you know your unicorn will come out cleanly.

Pop your unicorn in the lunchbox section that you've checked it fits.

Make a rainbow of fruits and vegetables. Go from one side of the box to the other. Start with red at one end, then add an orange food next to it, then yellow, and so on until you get to purple.

Top Tip!

Silicone cupcake cases can be super helpful here for adding an extra POP of colour. If one of your coloured foods isn't very bright, add it to a silicone case in that colour to make it stand out.

If you'd like to, you can add a few small cubes of cheese and put them in a little section of the lunchbox as a pot of gold at the end of the rainbow!

School Holiday Lunches

As we all know, just as you get you and your family into the routine of school and clubs, and bedtimes and packed lunches, another school holiday comes hurtling around the corner! Some days you might be sticking with packed lunches and holiday clubs while others will bring more relaxed mornings without the chaos of finding bags and shoes and water bottles, but it does mean you'll be feeding the kids six million times a day. So, this chapter is full of fun food ideas for days at home when food can be served hot or on a big family-sharing platter. Hope you enjoy!

Mini Pancake Muffins

Why not start the day with this cute and delicious breakfast idea, served in the middle of the table on a big board with lots of fruit? I promise it's so easy you don't even need to buy a pancake mix; you'll probably have most of these ingredients at home anyway. The ingredients listed below make 24 mini muffins, but if you only have a regular fairy cake tin, you'll get 12 of those instead (just adjust the cooking time slightly longer to ensure they're cooked through).

You'll need

- 150g self-raising flour
- 1 tsp baking powder
- 150ml milk
- 1 egg (large if you have it, if not medium will be fine)
- 2 tbsp sugar
- 30g butter (melted)
- OPTIONAL: a few drops of vanilla extract
- A variety of toppings: berries, peanut butter, small chunks of milk or white chocolate, sprinkles, mini marshmallows – or even chocolate and marshmallows for a scrummy s'mores vibe!

What to do

Preheat your oven to 160°C fan, then grease a mini muffin tin with a little butter or oil.

Mix the dry ingredients in a mixing bowl and whisk the wet ones in a jug.

Pour the wet mix into the bowl of dry ingredients and whisk until smooth.

Split the mixture between the 24 mini muffin spaces. Don't worry about filling them quite full; they'll make muffin tops – but the best of us have them!

Top with your chosen toppings and bake for 10 to 15 minutes until nicely risen and golden brown.

Top Tip!

Any chocolate chunks will sink, so add a few extra on top while the muffins are hot from the oven.

These muffins are extra delicious warm, but they can be tricky to remove from the tin until they've cooled a little . . . So, do as you wish! A thin metal teaspoon is best to lever them out if you want to eat them warm – simply loosen the edges first, then scoop under.

Once fully cooled, these can also be packed in a lunchbox, as a snack, or pop them in the fridge for one or two days and reheat gently in the microwave until piping hot.

Jam Donut Roll-Ups

Imagine you're six and your mum says you can have jam donuts for breakfast. You'd be so happy, right? Well, this breakfast brings all those vibes, but is much healthier. The ingredients below make two roll-ups for two toddlers or for one older child. You can simply double up the ingredients per extra child – or for yourself of course, if you fancy jam donuts for breakfast too!

You'll need

- 2 slices of bread
- Raspberry jam (or any other preferred flavour), or chocolate spread
- 1 egg (large or medium is fine)
- Butter – for the pan
- Granulated sugar – for sprinkling
- A splash of milk (a tablespoon or two, if you like to measure)
- OPTIONAL: a pinch of ground flaxseed

What to do

Lay your slices of bread on a chopping board, remove the crusts and roll flat with a rolling pin. Spread on your jam or chocolate spread and sprinkle over your ground flaxseed (if using).

In a large flat bowl (e.g. a pasta bowl, or a dinner plate with a lip), beat your egg and add a splosh of milk.

From one of the small ends, tightly roll the bread up like a Swiss roll.

Add the rolled-up bread to the egg mix, and coat all over, allowing it to soak a little while you heat up a non-stick frying pan on a medium heat.

Add a knob of butter to the pan and allow to melt. Add the roll-ups to the pan with the flappy edge down; this way it seals together. Once browned underneath, keep turning it over a little so it cooks all the way around.

Add some sugar to a bowl or tub that's just a little bigger than your rolled-up bread, then add the roll-ups to the sugar and shake the bowl to coat the roll-ups, like a donut!

Serve warm with some fresh fruit and a glass of milk. Perfect start to the day!

Easy DIY Pizza Bar

My kids love pizza and, compared to a slice of cheese on toast, pizza offers an opportunity for a lot more vegetables to make it onto their plates. Which is why DIY pizza is one of my go-to at home lunches!

This is one of those ideas that really works best if you get the kids involved in making their own. You can either simply let them create their own, or challenge them to make pizza art, or see if they'll try adding a little bit of something new to one corner of their DIY pizza. I tend to find that when they're involved in the decision making, they feel like they – rather than you – have chosen to try something new. (That's if they will try something. They won't always, and that's perfectly okay.)

You'll need

- **Pizza bases** in the form of sliced bread, bagels, pitta bread, mini naan breads, burger buns, English muffins, and so on.
- **Pizza sauce:** you can use passata or a little tomato puree mixed with water or ketchup to thin it out a little.
- **Pizza toppings:** tinned sweetcorn (or frozen, but cooked first), red onion, mushrooms, peppers, ham, cooked chicken, leftover sausages, pepperoni (a mini snack pepperoni cut into tiny circles works really well for these).
- **Pizza cheese:** mozzarella if you've planned ahead and have it in the fridge. If not, any grated cheese will be just as tasty.
- **Pizza sprinkles** by which I mean . . . oregano! Calling a scattering of dried herbs sprinkles can help fussy eaters by making them sound much less new and daunting. And adding the oregano will hopefully make the pizzas tastier, but can also help as an introduction to the flavour, which in turn can encourage children to accept it as a taste in other meals in the future.

What to do

Set out all the available ingredients either in a sectioned plate, a muffin tray or lots of little bowls.

Toast the underside of your pizza bases (slice bagels, muffins and pitta breads in half through the centre before toasting) in the grill or airfryer.

Call the kids to come and assemble their pizzas. They can practise spreading out the pizza sauce over their chosen base with the back of a teaspoon, or for little ones joining in they might like to use a pastry brush.

Next, they can add toppings and cheese in any order they like, plus special pizza sprinkles – aka oregano – if they'd like to.

Now you can pop the pizzas back under the grill, or into the airfryer at 200°C for 4 to 5 minutes or until the cheese is bubbling and the bread crusts are golden brown.

Cut into kid-sized pieces and let them enjoy their own pizza feast!

The Sandwich Express

This is my take on an idea I found in a book at my mother-in-law's house, and I thought it was too brilliant not to re-create. The original 1990s version was by Carole Handslip, but this is my 2020s version for fussy eaters.

Creating the Sandwich Express isn't for every day, but it can expose a fussy eater to lots of different fillings in a super fun, no pressure way. Fill the sandwiches with lots of different fillings (focusing on ones you think they'll have the most chance of enjoying), and offer them up as a sharing platter. Then you can sit together and explore the train and the new flavours together.

Even if they just have a play with the Sandwich Express and maybe simply take the smallest of nibbles (or even just a lick), it all helps in their fussy eater journey. For that alone, I promise the effort of creation will be worth it. And any leftovers can be stored in an airtight tub in the fridge and eaten by less fussy adults the following day.

You'll need

- 4 slices of bread
- Fillings of your choice (aim for 4 in total)
- Mini pepperoni
- Mini crackers
- Cucumber

> Reduce any potential fussy eater anxiety by including a mix of their favourite fillings alongside one or two new ones.
>
> **Top Tip!**

Some sandwich filler options to try

- Jam/marmalade – why not try a new flavour?
- Cheese spread/cream cheese
- Cheese
- Ham
- Peanut butter (alone or with jam)

What to do

Remove all the crusts. Cut each slice in half – like you usually would, from longer side to longer side) and use two halves to make one sandwich of each flavour.

Cut each sandwich into thirds so they're a sixth of an original slice of bread.

NOW TO ASSEMBLE YOUR TRAIN!

First, make your train engine with one sandwich at the front and three stacked behind.

A couple of inches behind this, make a carriage by stacking two sandwiches. Continue making three more carriages. You may need to curve around your board to get them all on.

Between each stack add a thin stick of cucumber (skin up) as the train's track.

Use your mini crackers to add wheels. You could stick them on with butter or cheese spread if your fussy eaters would accept, or simply balance them in place if you think any extra spread will cause upset.

And finally add some pepperoni funnels to the engine. Use a 1 cm(ish) slice at the front and a taller rounded end-piece just behind.

Top Tip!

For a party, place your train down the centre of the table and continue adding carriages to create as long a train as you wish!

Muffin Tray Lunch

Muffin tray lunches are the ultimate in lazy parenting that don't look lazy at all. In fact, they look super fancy! My favourite part about these brilliant lunches is the lack of mental load needed – you don't even need to think 'what on earth can I feed the kids today?' Instead, you can just grab a muffin tin, open the fridge and start chucking different food groups into the tray's different sections. A bit of this and a bit of that until the tray is full and you've covered fruit, veg, dairy, carbs and protein.

One muffin tray is perfect for a couple of kids, or you can put together and serve two trays (if you have them) for more kids. Or, you might want to use one tray alongside a 'main' element like a cheese toastie, or plate of little sandwiches.

The version here is a cheese toastie muffin tray lunch (which will serve two), but you can swap the toasties out for crackers with cheese and meats, fingers of toasted pitta breads and some dips – anything you have in the fridge.

You'll need

- A 12-hole muffin tin
- 4 slices of bread
- Cheese
- Butter
- 2 to 3 fruits
- 2 to 3 veggies
- 2 to 3 snacks (a mix of sweet and savoury)

What to do

Butter all your slices of bread then stack them butter sides together on a board.

Add sliced or grated cheese to two non-buttered sides of the bread.

Lift the top slice of bread off its partner, and into a hot frying pan on a medium-high heat. If you have a large enough frying pan you should be able to get both sandwiches in at once. If not, cook one at a time in a smaller pan.

Top with the other slice of bread, butter side up.

After a couple of minutes, lift the corner of the sandwich to see if it's golden-brown underneath, then flip over and toast the other side too.

Once cooked, tip onto a cooling rack to cool a little, then cut into mini sandwiches. I remove the crusts, cut the sandwich in half, then each half into four little pieces.

Add your mini toasties to the muffin tray, dotting them around so no two adjacent sections are the same, then continue filling up the remaining spaces with your other food groups. Serve with some little plates and some mini tongs (if you have them) so everyone can serve themselves.

These are really simple to make allergy friendly. Just use gluten-free pastry (remember to check ingredients for any additional allergens), then brush with non-dairy milk before baking.

Top Tip!

Hidden Veggie Sausage Swirls

What's more comforting than a hot sausage roll? Here's how to make them extra fun by rolling them into swirls AND you can add those all-important hidden vegetables too, and no one will ever know!

You'll need

- 1 sheet of puff pastry
- 375g pack of sausage meat (ensure gluten free if needed)
- 1 carrot (start small for fussy eaters)
- A little milk

What to do

Preheat your oven to 200°C fan and take your pastry out of the fridge so that it's at room temperature when you need it.

Meanwhile, pop your sausage meat in a mixing bowl and finely grate your carrot on top. Squish it all together until the carrot is evenly distributed so no one will even notice it's there.

Unroll your pastry onto a chopping board, keeping it on the backing paper. Add the sausage meat mixture on top and press it out until you have an even layer over the top of the pastry.

Roll it up as tightly as possible – roll from the long edge for more, smaller swirls, or from the short edge for fewer, bigger ones.

Use a large, serrated knife (e.g. a breadknife) to cut into slices about 1.5 to 2 cm thick.

> **Top Tip!**
> Saw slowly with your serrated knife without pressing too hard. This will give you nice round swirls rather than squished wonky ones. If you're finding them tricky to cut, pop them back in the fridge to chill for 5 to 10 minutes then try again.

Move your beautifully cut swirls onto a non-stick tray, or lined baking sheet, and brush with a little milk.

Pop in the oven for 17 to 20 minutes, or until golden brown and the meat is fully cooked through. (Use a meat thermometer if you have one. If not, cut a swirl open across the middle and check it's piping hot right through to the centre, with no pink meat visible.)

Serve warm at home or cool fully before packing into lunchboxes. You might well find that the adults in your family are pretty keen on these too.

> **Top Tip!**
> To mix things up a bit, try making these thinner and crispier by squashing the swirls flatter once on the baking tray, before brushing with milk. This also helps you reshape any wonky ones that weren't behaving when being sliced. No one will ever know!

Toaster Wraps

This lunch is a love story between a cheese toastie and a quesadilla! If your child likes either, then try them on this. It's perfect when you need lunch on the table sharpish, or if you have a child who enjoys getting involved in the kitchen. Younger kids can assemble them from prepped ingredients and will just need a little help removing it hot from the toaster, but older kids can make this one independently.

You'll need

- 1 tortilla wrap (full sized not mini)
- Cheese
- Any additional ingredients they like, e.g. some tomato puree for a pizza vibe, tomatoes, onion, pepper, ham, pepperoni

What to do

Lay your wrap out flat and add your toppings to the centre third of the wrap, leaving a small gap in the middle, like this:

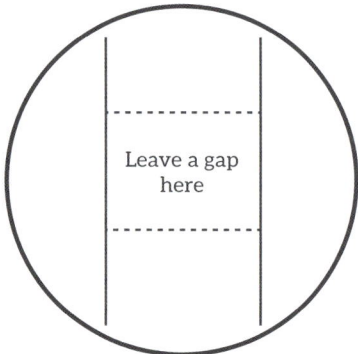

Now fold the two sides into the middle.

Then fold the whole wrap in half, making a neat little pocket.

Place your pocket in the toaster, with the folded edge at the bottom, and the open flaps to the top. This is very important – or you'll be in a right (and rather dangerous) mess.

Toast until the wrap is browned and the cheese inside is melted. Enjoy!

Rainbow Toasties

I dare you to blow the kids' minds with these cheese toasties that stretch and ooze the colours of the rainbow!

You'll need

- 2 slices of bread
- A handful of grated mozzarella (or a mix of mozzarella and Cheddar)
- 4 different food colouring gels
- Butter or spreadable butter

What to do

Butter both slices of bread then stack them, buttered sides together, on a board.

Split your grated cheese into 4 small dishes, add a squirt of different coloured food colouring to each dish and mix with a spoon to coat all of the cheese.

Add the cheese to the non-buttered side of the bread, from top to bottom in rows of each colour.

Lift the top slice of bread off its partner, and put it into a hot frying pan on a medium-high heat.

Top with the other slice of bread, buttered side up.

After a couple of minutes, lift the corner of the sandwich to see if it's golden-brown underneath, then flip over and toast the other side too.

Once cooked, tip onto a cooling rack for a couple of minutes so the cheese isn't too piping hot, but keeping the bread from going soggy while waiting.

Cut into two triangles* and serve to mightily impressed kids!

* This is important because cutting across diagonally, into triangles, reveals all the colours of your rainbow toastie.

How to Platter Anything and Everything

Kids' food doesn't always have to be something new and exciting, but it can feel so DULL serving up the same thing day after day. I find the easiest way to mix up mundane lunches is to serve everything on a board together and let the kids help themselves. If you're worried that they will just eat the fun stuff and not what their body needs in terms of nutrition, then have a low-key chat about it first and remind everyone that they need to eat at least some fruit and veg. Try not to go overboard with the rules or it rather takes away the idea of this being a fun, easy and straightforward lunch option for everyone.

Three rules to guarantee a good platter

1. **The fuller the better!** You're better off with a smaller board (or plate) and cramming it full. I think this always looks way more fun than empty space. My favourite board is a circular 30 cm board, with a 25 cm diameter space for the food. I find this plenty big enough for my two kids. Equally, if your child is likely to worry about different foods touching, you might need to space everything out a little more. However, over time you may be able to squeeze some foods a little closer together; as with everything, it all depends on your child and their responses.
2. **Variety is key!** Try to add as many different foods as possible. Different colours, different shapes, different textures. Hitting all your food groups helps with the variety, so add a couple of choices of fruits, veggies, proteins, dairy and carbs.
3. **Make it mini!** I don't know quite why this is, but food is just way more fun when it's mini! Cut sandwiches smaller than usual, either with a knife into mini squares or triangles, or get your cutters out and add a few shapes too.

Top Tip!

If you really don't think the kids will make a balanced choice if left to their own devices, then plate up mini versions on small plates for the same personalised platter effect.

What to do

Grab your board or plate and add three small dishes: maybe some leftover glass pudding pots you've been saving for absolutely no reason, some silicone cupcake cases, or any mini plastic tubs that you have kicking about. And for this, you don't even need to try and find their lids – whoop!

Add the tubs to your board: it doesn't really matter where, as long as they are nicely spread out.

Start with your 'main' foods. Think sandwiches, scones, crackers, etc, and add these in a C shape around one or two of the tubs, around a section of the edge of the board, or even as a snake coming across the board. Anywhere you like, but with the aim of keeping each food together and in an interesting shape.

Now add some colour with your fruit and veg. Place little handfuls of these dotted around the board. If you're using cut fruits, remember they might be a bit juicy so use your little tubs: that way they don't make other foods wet and soggy.

Add your protein options in little piles. Present them in ways that are easy to nibble – little cubes or slices of cheese, ham rolled up and cut into bite-sized swirls. Add shop-bought mini cheeses, or other snacky picnic foods. Again, keep them in small piles and scatter them around the board.

If you find you have a larger amount of some foods, then you can dot them around in two to three smaller piles, as this always looks more appealing and attractive than a single big lump of one thing.

Add some foods to your tubs if you haven't already. If your children like dips, then the tubs are great for that. If not, add anything else little that might need a container, or split treats between pots and let the kids know that they can have one treat pot each.

Fill in any gaps with any mini foods you have to hand: breakfast cereals, pretzels, a few blueberries, sweets or chocolate shapes. If you have too many gaps to be filled in by a few extras then you'll need to add some more of the main food groups until your board is mostly filled, then come back to this step.

Take a photo of your marvellous creation, then serve to the kids with individual plates for them to plate up with their own choices. If you have mini tongs then let them serve themselves and each other with these. If not, just let them dive in!

Fun at Home

Playing with their food can really help a fussy eater to gain confidence in trying new things. If you can interest them in cooking dinner, then that's awesome, but if you need to start with fun food, then it's absolutely fine to do that too. For some fussy eaters, even trying a new biscuit can really feel like a big deal – so, for me, the plan is to familiarise them with the idea of trying foods rather than rejecting them on sight.

Use this chapter to bring foodie fun to a rainy day, or as an idea for a cheap and cheerful playdate activity, but also take a moment to feel smug about exposing your children to new food ideas safe in the knowledge that it will all be part of helping them build their confidence around food.

What do you call an activity that doubles as a snack once the kids have finished making it? That's correct, they are 'snacktivities' – and that's how this chapter ends. The beauty of these is that they should buy you a moment of peace to clean up while the kids eat it and before they're letting you know that they're bored – or hungry – again . . . we've all had those days, right?

Playdate Platters

Feeding the troops on a playdate doesn't have to be daunting. If you don't know the child so well, I think it's a really good idea to speak to, or text, their parent or carer a few days before and ask what they're most likely to be happy eating at yours. Check, too, whether they have any food allergies or intolerances to be aware of.

As a child, I was a fussy eater myself, and I can still remember the feeling of dread at going for dinner at a friend's house and being served something that I desperately didn't want to try, especially not in front of someone else's family. So, with this in mind, I like to serve Playdate Platters when we have friends round. I'll cook up some crowd-pleasers and pop all the options on a big board in the centre of the table and let everyone pick and choose the things they like. Does it matter too much if a child doesn't eat any veg one day while at someone else's house? Not at all! But what does matter to me is that the child felt comfortable, enjoyed what they did eat, generally had a nice time and would like to come back again.

You'll need

- A big board – either a bread board, chopping board, a clean tray or your biggest dinner plate
- Crowd-pleaser dinner items: chicken nuggets, fish fingers, sausages, chips, pizza in small slices, sausage rolls – you know the drill
- Pickable healthy bits: sliced fruit, veggie sticks, tiny bowls of peas or sweetcorn
- Tongs or serving spoons – we want to share the food not the germs
- A few little treats if you're feeling a bit extra

What to do

Cook enough food for everyone to pick and mix what they want.

Add everything to the sharing board either in big piles of each item, or portion certain foods like chips out into silicone muffin cases, or small plastic tumblers, so the kids can each take one and no one will miss out.

Lay everything out on the table then call the kids to let them know dinner is served! Let them all know they can serve themselves, that it might be good to eat some fruit or veg if there's anything they like, but that you won't make them. Then leave them to it. If you're like me, you'll enjoy overhearing snippets of their chit chat as they eat together – it's like a glimpse into those school lunchtimes we see nothing of.

Pick 'n' Mix Snack Bar

If you're bored of serving a million snacks a day (hello school holidays!), or you simply want to mix up lunchtime and make it less mundane – grab a muffin tray and as many different foods as you have, and create a bright, colourful tiny buffet for the kids. This works especially well for sharing, because you can include foods you know one child doesn't like and it helps expose them to the food, without any pressure of eating it – it's there 'because it's for someone else', which makes its presence feel a lot easier. If you're serving this idea to just one child and you want to try this approach of including something new, then you can always add some things you like and join in eating with them.

If you aren't a baker and don't have a muffin tray, you could grab a cheap second hand one just for this idea. I see them so often in the charity shops so you should be able to find one easily enough. Look out for a deep muffin one rather than a shallow fairy-cake one if you want to use it to serve a couple of people.

You'll need

- 2 to 3 fruits
- 2 to 3 veggies
- 2 to 3 protein rich foods
- 2 to 3 grains/carbohydrate rich foods
- 1 to 2 treats

What to do

When choosing the foods to serve, try and include as many different colours as possible as it helps to make the overall tray look more fun and exciting! A few colourful fruits and some tactical Smarties can make a big difference.

Top Tip!
The prep for this is absolutely minimal. You don't even need to get everything out before you begin. Simply grab your muffin tray and start filling up the sections.

Try not to put two foods of the same colour next to each other (this might turn into a bit of a puzzle by the end, admittedly), and if you think it's all looking a big beige, mix it up with a few colourful silicone muffin cases dotted around.

If you haven't got any silicone muffin cases try cutting a few circles out from colourful serviettes – of course, this works best with dry foods.

Top Tip!

Snowman Hot Chocolate

Nothing beats the winter blues quite like a hot chocolate. The warm hug between your hands, the rich milky chocolate – *sigh* . . .

I make our hot chocolates with milk rather than water, as my children don't drink milk often, and I like to get some milky goodness into them (along with all the sugar, I know). If you're making it for younger children, you can use less chocolate to reduce their sugar intake. Remember that marshmallows can be a choking hazard for little ones, so act accordingly.

You'll need (for 1 big kid, or 2 smaller ones)

- 200ml milk (we like whole milk best)
- 15g white chocolate
- A drop of vanilla extract
- A few white mini marshmallows
- Edible ink pens
- OPTIONAL: squirty cream

What to do

First make your snowman marshmallows by drawing black dots onto the marshmallows with your edible ink pens as snowman eyes and mouth. Then grab your orange pen and lay the nib flat and stroke sideways, to make a carrot nose. You'll need a few snowmen per cup so keep drawing till you get bored! Set your snowmen aside.

Next, add your milk, white chocolate and vanilla to a small pan and stir while the chocolate melts and the milk warms.

Pour the milk into either one normal-sized mug, or a couple of small kids' ones, and top up with cold milk until it's a safe drinking temperature for your child(ren).

Add squirty cream if you're using it, then carefully pop your snowmen marshmallows on top with the faces up – don't be tempted to just sprinkle them or your hard work will be dunked face down in cream – and your own face will be sad!

Top Tip!

If you don't have kids' mugs, then cheap espresso cups – for toddlers past the throwing stage – make for a mega cute hot chocolate experience.

Movie Afternoon Snacks

I love a family cinema trip as much as the next person, but I also love curling up on the sofa with my crew, drawing the curtains, shutting out the world and snuggling together eating snacks – while getting lost in a movie! These snack trays are perfect for making your movie afternoon feel that little bit more special. Ask the kids to make tickets or search some free printable ones online and give them to the kids to colour while you sort the snacks. By giving everyone their own tray, there's no arguments over sharing, which means you will all enjoy the peace of the film much better than if you simply open some packets of sweets and hope for the best!

Safety First!

Popcorn is a choking hazard for younger children, so swap it out for age-appropriate fun snacks in the same containers so they can safely join in with any bigger siblings.

You'll need (per child)

- An empty cereal box (either start saving these for the future or decant some half-empty boxes into Tupperware)
- 1 plastic bowl and 1 tumbler (plastic is better because it's lighter, but if you're past that phase and no longer have any plastic ones, choose your lightest regular crockery)
- 1 drinks bottle or cup with a non-spill lid and straw
- Popcorn
- Sweets

What to do

Take your cereal box and reseal the open end so you have a solid box.

If you're feeling fancy, or you intend to reuse these trays, wrap the box in some wrapping paper or plain paper so the kids can decorate them, making sure to glue the paper to the top of the box so it doesn't flap when you cut into it in the next step.

Place your bowl, cup and bottle where you want them to sit on top of the box, then draw around them so you know where to cut.

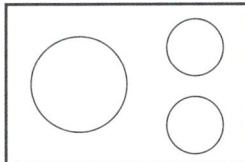

Next, carefully stab one blade of your scissors into the centre of one circle, then cut outwardly until just past your circular line. Continue cutting around, making the hole you cut just a few millimetres bigger than the circle you drew.

With all three circle shapes cut, carefully slot your bowl, cup and bottle into their spaces and push down until their bases sit on the bottom of the box.

Add popcorn or crisps to the bowl, a few sweets or other treats to the cup, and add a drink in their bottle. Hand out the trays and delight in feeling like the most fun parent that ever there was!

Broken Biscuit Rocky Road

Do you ever open the snack cupboard and find umpteen packets with just one or two lonely biscuits inside? I'm not sure who is opening new packets before finishing the old ones, but in our house, we definitely get to the point where the cupboard is overrun by loads of half-empty packets.

So, one rainy Wednesday afternoon, I decided to do something about it. I opened the snack cupboard and scooped up all those odds and ends that no one was eating, threw them all in a bowl and turned them into BROKEN BISCUIT ROCKY ROAD!

And, you know what, I don't think my family have ever loved anything more! Even better, it really is super easy. No baking required. Just melt, crush, stir and chill (the biscuits and you both) before chopping the resulting Rocky Road into chunks.

I admit, this is probably not ideal for school lunches, but it is the perfect treat on the walk home – maybe not in the car, though, unless you enjoy chocolatey, sticky handprints on everything . . .

You'll need

FOR PEOPLE WHO LIKE SPECIFICS
- 200g biscuits/cake bars etc
- 200g milk chocolate
- 100g butter
- 2–3 tbsp golden syrup
- 100g tasty extras like mini marshmallows, raisins or sultanas and broken up pretzels

FOR PEOPLE WHO LIKE TO FLY BY THE SEAT OF THEIR PANTS
- Put an empty bowl on the scales and unwrap all your biscuits/cake bars and chuck them in. How much does it weigh? **Remember this number!**
- Scavenge for the **same weight** of milk chocolate (this is an excellent excuse to use up any old Easter eggs, or Christmas chocolate you might have lying around)
- Butter (you'll need approximately **half the weight** of biscuits)
- Golden syrup – a good squirt or dollop from the tin
- Tasty extras: mini marshmallows, raisins or sultanas and broken up pretzels

What to do

Line a baking tray with baking paper. You'll need a tray that's a couple of centimetres deep, and about 20 cm square. Don't worry if your tin is a bit too big, as you can squash all your mixture up one end fairly easily.

Break up your biscuits and cake bars into small chunks and set aside.

Place the chocolate and butter in a large heatproof mixing bowl and place over a saucepan containing a little water. Gently heat the water and allow the steam to melt the chocolate and butter.

> You can also melt the chocolate in the microwave, just keep the power down low – I find the defrost setting works best – and stir every 20 to 30 seconds.
>
> *Top Tip!*

Add the golden syrup and stir. (If measuring the syrup, then warm the spoon you use with boiling water first; it makes the whole process a lot more manageable.)

Tip in the biscuit cake mix and any tasty extras. Then fold until evenly mixed.

Pour into the lined baking tray and spread the mixture out evenly.

It doesn't matter too much about the size or shape of your tin, just choose anything you have with sides (about 2 cm tall). Pour the mixture in and, if the tin is too large, push the mixture all to one side to keep it nice and thick.

Top Tip!

Pop in the fridge for a couple of hours until set, then cut into chunks. Serve what you're eating and keep the rest in a tub in the fridge for the next couple of days. My family don't let it last very long in my house!

Any Excuse for a Tea Party

Use these ideas separately or together depending on the mood of the day. I love a tea pot or pretty jug full of hot chocolate as an excuse to sit up at the table together after school and enjoy a comforting drink and a good chat about their day. It feels like going out to a café, but cheap and easy, and at home!

And then sometimes life calls for a proper tea party. Grab a load of teddies or dollies and sit them up at the table. Set the table with a flourish and give everyone a little cup or mug. Then fill your favourite teapot or jug with some hot (but not too hot) chocolate and have a proper little tea party together.

HOT CHOCOLATE TEA POT . . . For little kids, espresso mugs are perfect (perhaps save your best ones until they're past that toddler throwing stage). For bigger kids, collect mismatched china teacups, saucers and little plates from charity shops or car boot sales – to add a real fancy tea party vibe!

Top Tip!

Hot Chocolate Tea Pot

You'll need

- EITHER: your favourite hot chocolate
- OR: homemade hot chocolate – 250ml whole milk, flat teaspoon of cocoa powder and a heaped teaspoon of brown sugar
- OR: see page 134 for my homemade 'Snowman' white chocolate hot chocolate recipe
- A teapot or jug
- Lots of little cups or mugs
- Teddies, dolls or real-life friends and family
- OPTIONAL: squirty cream and marshmallows (beware of choking hazards with younger kids)

What to do

Make your hot chocolate either in a pan on the hob, or in a jug in the microwave, and pour into the tea pot to allow the kids to serve.

For little kids make sure the hot chocolate is only warm and not hot.

For bigger kids you can adjust the temperature and fullness of the pot, as you see fit.

> Be careful not to overfill the tea pot to allow for any over-zealous pouring technique!
>
> **Top Tip!**

Tea Party

Use the instructions below to make your own tiered cake plate, then add a few mini sandwiches, some fruit and mini biscuits and you'll have yourself a display worthy of a full-on fancy tea party. Of course, if you already have a tiered cake plate – perhaps picked up in a charity shop or a cardboard one from a bargain store – then you can use that instead.

You'll need

- 2 paper plates (plain or patterned)
- 1 paper cup
- A hot glue gun. PVA glue works fine but just takes a bit longer to dry, so make in advance
- A colourful array of tea party snacks

What to do

Take one of the paper plates and cut off an inch or so all around the edge. Flip your plate over and there may be a circle fold marked in the card – cut around that line. If not, then cut freehand if you're a daredevil, or use another small plate to draw a circle to follow with your scissors, for a nice and neat end result.

Run a line of glue around the top rim of the paper cup, then turn it upside down and stick it in the centre of the bigger (uncut) plate.

Run a line of glue around the base of the cup (that is now facing up), then stick the smaller, cut plate on top.

Leave to dry, then add any snacks you'd like to serve at your tea party.

Snack Necklace

These are the ultimate portable snack for school-age kids! Let the kids get creative designing and making their necklaces, then once they're ready they can be eaten anywhere – on a family walk, in the car on a long journey, or even curled up on the sofa in front of a film.

> Remember anything juicy or wet will be very messy to wear, so stick to dry foods.
>
> *Top Tip!*

You'll need

- Snacky foods with holes in: any hoop cereals, hoop crisps, pretzels, mini ring biscuits, Taralli (little hooped breadstick-type snacks), dried apple rings, mints with holes in
- Any additional foods to try and make holes in. You can use the end of a chopstick or skewer to gently drill a hole though dried fruits or mini crackers, etc – this works best with dry but not too snappable snacks
- Food safe string or butcher's twine – cut in 50 to 60 cm (approx.) lengths
- A clean freezer clip

What to do

Set out all the foods you want to use in small bowls, or in a sectioned plate.

Cut your string to length and, for younger children, attach a freezer clip to one end to stop everything falling off as they add more.

Let the kids add the foods they like to create their own necklaces – encourage free expression or pattern making.

Once complete, tie the ends of your string together so they can wear the necklace long and loose.

> Clearly, there is a strangulation risk here. Don't let anyone tie their necklaces tight and make sure all children are supervised while wearing them.
>
> *Safety First!*

Lazy Baking

The back of a teaspoon is often easiest for small hands to spread icing with.

Top Tip!

Sometimes you want to be a mum who bakes cakes and biscuits with the kids in a way that means they'll build a lovely store of wholesome memories to treasure forever. And sometimes you just don't have the energy . . .

Enter – Lazy Baking!

There's minimal set up and no cook time. This is how you do it.

1. Simply grab some plain shop-bought biscuits (in our house, we like digestives or rich tea the best) and all the sprinkles you can find.
2. Let the kids get creative! Their brief is to make a couple each then eat them for their snack.
3. Meanwhile . . . you drink a hot cuppa in peace.

You'll need

- 2 biscuits per child
- Icing*
- Sprinkles and sweets for decoration

What to do

Pop everything on a board. Or, for less mess, give each child a couple of biscuits and a small amount of icing and a quota of sprinkles or sweets on their own plate and let them get creative.

* Either mix a couple of tablespoons of icing sugar with a little water and food colouring to make your own icing, or cheat even further and use chocolate spread or peanut butter!

Rainbow Toast

This idea went NUTS on Instagram in summer 2023, so if you haven't tried it yet, first — where have you even been? And second, this is your sign! Obviously, you wouldn't want to serve up food-colouring toast every day of the week, but as a fun snacktivity, it's always a big win in our house.

You'll need

- Bread (lightly coloured rather than wholemeal)
- Milk
- A few food colourings
- Some food-safe paint brushes (or for little kids, fingertips would do the trick)

What to do

Grab a few little dishes, or a plate with a few separate sections, and add a little bit of milk to each.

Drop in a small squirt of food colouring to each dish and mix until properly mixed.

Now the kids can use the paint brushes to dip and gently dab the bread to paint their designs.

When your little artists are finished, pop the bread into the toaster* on the lowest heat setting and toast to set the colours — keep a careful watch so the toast doesn't brown and ruin the artwork.

Once ready, let them eat it plain, or with butter and/or honey, as a see-through topping. Serve with some fruit and a yoghurt, and let them enjoy their creations for a snack.

* If they've gotten a little over-enthusiastic adding their colourful milk to the bread, and it's become rather soggy, it'll be safer to toast it under the grill or in the airfryer, rather than in an electric toaster . . .

Chocolate Lollies

Last summer, we went to a chocolate factory in the Yorkshire Dales. It was literally my idea of heaven with taps of melted chocolate pouring constantly – I'd like one of those in my kitchen, if I'm honest . . . One highlight of the trip was when they showed the kids how to make chocolate lollies. Theirs were made with proper tempered chocolate, whereas this is very much the DIY at home version, but I promise any chocolate lover will LOVE this one too.

These lollies would also be fabulous as a party activity, as long as you have enough fridge space to put them all in flat, without them touching while they set.

You'll need (makes 4 big lollies, or more smaller ones)

- 200g of your chosen chocolate (milk, white or dark)
- Lolly sticks (the white paper ones, rather than wooden ice lolly ones)
- Baking paper on a solid surface that you can transfer to the fridge, like a chopping board or oven tray
- Mini marshmallows, small sweets or sprinkles to decorate

Top Tip!

If you're planning on making them at a party, buy some little cellophane bags in advance, then you can pop them over each lolly at the end of the party, tie with a ribbon and ta-dah! Your guests have just made their own party favour – and you don't have to faff about with plastic tat for party bags. Double win!

What to do

Put your decorations in little separate bowls in readiness for when the decorating chaos descends later.

Use a pencil to draw around a small glass, on the baking paper, to make 4 circles (a few centimetres apart in case the lollies spread more than expected).

Flip the baking paper over so your chocolate doesn't get pencil in it, and pop it on a chopping board or baking tray.

TO MELT YOUR CHOCOLATE
EITHER: heat a few centimetres of water in a saucepan and melt your chocolate in a heatproof bowl over it as the water simmers gently.

OR: place your broken up chocolate in a heatproof bowl in the microwave on the defrost setting for 30 seconds, stir then repeat in 15 to 20 second bursts, stirring each time until melted.

Once the chocolate is melted, transfer it to a small jug to make it easier for the children to pour it out.

Top Tip!

If you're using a small Pyrex jug, pop it in a bowl of warm water to heat up a little, otherwise the chocolate might start to set in the jug before it is poured.

Pour the chocolate into the centre of one circle until it spreads nearly to the edges, stop just before and let it settle. Repeat for the second circle.

If your chocolate lollies haven't poured very evenly you can swirl the baking tray in a circular motion, while it is flat on the table, to help distribute the chocolate more evenly.

Put the top couple of centimetres of the lolly stick into the chocolate then twist it over to fully coat the stick and make it more secure.

Now everyone can go wild decorating with sprinkles and sweeties.

Top Tip!

If you're doing this as a party activity, don't forget to add each child's name to their baking paper, so you know whose lolly is whose at the end.

Once they're done, pop the whole thing in the fridge for around 15 to 20 minutes to set fully before peeling off the paper and enjoying!

The Happiest of Meals

This was very much a lockdown tradition that started when we had no choice but to make our own fun at home. But even out of lockdown, there are still plenty of days when you're feeling stuck at home and just need something different and fun to do with the kids. If today is one of those days, why not give this idea a whirl?

If your kids are old enough, then you can get them involved in cutting and sticking – and even decorating – their meal containers while you crack on with whatever you need to be doing. Or surprise younger kids with your wonderful homemade creation – made so much easier with this printable template (see QR code).

You'll need (per child)

- 2 sheets A4 thin card (colour of your choice)
- Scissors
- Double-sided sticky tape to make the boxes
- Chicken/veggie nuggets OR a burger and bun
- Chips of your choice: we like fries for authenticity!
- OPTIONAL: a small toy (keep an eye out for offers, or odds and ends that you pick up in the charity shops)
- OPTIONAL: any leftover sauce packets you've saved

If you don't have double-sided sticky tape, a glue stick and some clothes pegs to hold the boxes together while the glue dries, works too.

Top Tip!

Scan me!

Scan this QR code or type the URL below into your browser.

https://blackandwhitepublishing.com/pages/the-lunchbox-mama

What to do – to prep your box

Follow the QR code and download your printable box templates. You'll find templates for burger boxes, trays for nuggets and containers for chips, so take your children's orders before printing what you need!

Cut around the solid lines, and fold any dashed lines.

If your card is fairly thick, a quick score with some scissors against a ruler will make for a much neater end product.

Top Tip!

Tape or glue your containers together and either set them aside or pass to your children to decorate with stickers. If you want the kids to colour their boxes, I recommend doing this before assembling.

Cook your food as per the instructions on the packets. Or if you want to use these fun containers to help your children try homemade nuggets why not try our favourite cornflake-coated chicken nuggets? Here is the recipe!

Cornflake Chicken Nuggets

You'll need

- Chicken breast (whole, mini fillets, or pre-chopped are fine)
- 1 egg
- Plain flour (gluten free if needed)
- A few handfuls of cornflakes
- OPTIONAL: flavourings such as garlic granules, paprika, parmesan or just salt and pepper

What to do

Preheat your oven to 180°C fan.

Find three flat bowls. To one, add your egg and beat. To another add your flour mixed with any additional flavourings. And in the third crush your cornflakes with your hands until they're the size of chunky breadcrumbs.

Now take a couple of non-stick trays, or baking sheets with non-stick tray liners, and lay them out ready on your work surface.

Cut your chicken breast to your desired shape.

Dunk the chicken first in the flour and coat all over, then into the egg mix, and finally into the cornflakes until fully coated.

Spread the nuggets or strips out onto your baking trays and bake in the oven for 20 minutes (flipping after 10 minutes), until they're golden brown and cooked through fully.

Top Tip!

Small nuggets might work best with fussy eaters who don't yet love non-processed chicken. Once mine grew to love these nuggets we progressed to long strips of chicken which have less coating per bite, which begins to gradually wean them onto non-coated chicken too.

Top Tip!

It works best to do a few nuggets at a time. But if you're short on time, you can always bung all the chicken into each bowl at once and just stir until everything is pretty much coated.

Happy Lunchboxing!

Rachel x

Thank you!

There are so many people I need and want to thank for helping make this book a reality. It's honestly the dream I never dared to dream and I'm so proud to call myself a published author!

First and foremost, thank YOU for trusting me enough to buy this book! I hope it helps make packing lunches a little less stressful, and a lot more fun. Please always send or tag me in photos on Instagram – I love to see you enjoying my ideas – tag @thelunchbox.mama.

Thank you to my online community. To everyone who has followed me on Instagram, whether you've been there from the beginning, through lockdown, since starting school or however you found me – without your support this book would never have happened. Thank you for being the most supportive group; I can't tell you what it means to know I always have a group of amazing mum-friends in my phone that I can ask all sorts of random advice from on my stories – you are honestly my favourite thing about this job!

Thank you to my children, who made my biggest life ambition, to be a mother, come true. I am grateful for you every day and I hope that me writing this book shows you that you can do anything you set your mind to – and I will always support you every step of the way, as you've supported me through this crazy year! I love you both more than you'll ever know.

Thank you to my husband, Alex, who believes in me more than I ever believe in myself. Sometimes, I only realise what a big deal some of my achievements are when I see them through your eyes.

Thank you to my mum who always made us 'surprise ice creams' and brought me up with fun food, which is the basis of my Instagram and now my book! And to my mother-in-law who told me it would be okay to quit my job and be a stay-at-home mum for a while, for assuring me that something would come from being at home with my children – how did you know!

Thank you to everyone I'm lucky enough to call my friend. To the best group of besties, who love to chat as much as I do and who have listened and supported me through my ups and downs (and many meltdowns): Hannah for ALWAYS getting it, Elaine for the walks and hours on the phone, Jo for all the milky tea (and cake) and endless support, Chelsey for walking this journey with me, always a phone call away, and Sophia for the baby steps that got me started. And my insta-foodie community, who all voice-noted me the most amazing advice about this journey you've walked before me – I could not have done this without you: Ciara, Kate, Grace, Simone, Laura, Casey, Amy, Becky and Sarah. Thank you!

And finally; to Ali, for sending that DM saying, have you ever considered writing a book? – thank you for this amazing opportunity and for being so invested from day one. To Emma, who gently removed hundreds of exclamation points from my writing and helped me turn my ideas into a real book. To Susie, the most amazing photographer who gave me the best and craziest week ever, for being so wonderful with my children and making a stressful week the best memory for us all. And to Kate, my book agent, for always having the most down to earth advice and making everything okay every time I spun a little!

"When my lunch looks nice it makes my tummy nice, I love heart sandwiches" – Rumaisah, age 4

"Your page has made food fun again for my family" – Ola

"I love the inspiration on how to introduce new things, or just cut food in a different way" – Tasha

"You've made our lunches much more creative and exciting whilst still quick, easy, affordable and healthy – WIN!" – Em

Inspiring

"Great ideas to help jazz up food!" – Catherine

"Gives me lots of foodie inspiration in a simple yet fun way!" – Naomi

"I love your page as it makes me feel better about my daughter being such a fussy eater" – Lesley

"You've given me great ideas for lunchboxes especially using the yumboxes" – Lisa

"You've helped me with new inspiration for what to try when boredom sets in for my 2-year-old" – Amy

Encouraging

"It's good to have accounts like yours that I can easily hop over to and get some quick inspiration" – Sonia

"Veggies taste nicer when they're cut like a star" – Thea, age 9

"I'm always taking your ideas on how to present new foods and the idea of exposure and I'm a true convert. It does work after many many months of persistence!! Your sandwich ideas finally worked on my little girl... makes life when out and about soooo much easier" – Jessica

"Realistic support, great ideas and at times a genuine lifeline!" – Jo

"You've given me the confidence to go with my gut instinct with my child's eating and relationship with food" – Sarah

"You've given me great ideas for lunchboxes" – Lisa

"I can't wait to open my lunchbox and see what ideas mummy got from lunchbox mama" – Imogen, age 8

"It helped me realise it's not just 'my kid'" – Molly